C-2358 CAREER EXAMINATION SERIES

This is your
PASSBOOK for...

Transportation Assistant

Test Preparation Study Guide
Questions & Answers

COPYRIGHT NOTICE

This book is SOLELY intended for, is sold ONLY to, and its use is RESTRICTED to individual, bona fide applicants or candidates who qualify by virtue of having seriously filed applications for appropriate license, certificate, professional and/or promotional advancement, higher school matriculation, scholarship, or other legitimate requirements of education and/or governmental authorities.

This book is NOT intended for use, class instruction, tutoring, training, duplication, copying, reprinting, excerption, or adaptation, etc., by:

1) Other publishers
2) Proprietors and/or Instructors of "Coaching" and/or Preparatory Courses
3) Personnel and/or Training Divisions of commercial, industrial, and governmental organizations
4) Schools, colleges, or universities and/or their departments and staffs, including teachers and other personnel
5) Testing Agencies or Bureaus
6) Study groups which seek by the purchase of a single volume to copy and/or duplicate and/or adapt this material for use by the group as a whole without having purchased individual volumes for each of the members of the group
7) Et al.

Such persons would be in violation of appropriate Federal and State statutes.

PROVISION OF LICENSING AGREEMENTS – Recognized educational, commercial, industrial, and governmental institutions and organizations, and others legitimately engaged in educational pursuits, including training, testing, and measurement activities, may address request for a licensing agreement to the copyright owners, who will determine whether, and under what conditions, including fees and charges, the materials in this book may be used them. In other words, a licensing facility exists for the legitimate use of the material in this book on other than an individual basis. However, it is asseverated and affirmed here that the material in this book CANNOT be used without the receipt of the express permission of such a licensing agreement from the Publishers. Inquiries re licensing should be addressed to the company, attention rights and permissions department.

All rights reserved, including the right of reproduction in whole or in part, in any form or by any means, electronic or mechanical, including photocopying, recording, or by any information storage and retrieval system, without permission in writing from the Publisher.

Copyright © 2025 by
National Learning Corporation

212 Michael Drive, Syosset, NY 11791
(516) 921-8888 • www.passbooks.com
E-mail: info@passbooks.com

PASSBOOK® SERIES

THE *PASSBOOK® SERIES* has been created to prepare applicants and candidates for the ultimate academic battlefield – the examination room.

At some time in our lives, each and every one of us may be required to take an examination – for validation, matriculation, admission, qualification, registration, certification, or licensure.

Based on the assumption that every applicant or candidate has met the basic formal educational standards, has taken the required number of courses, and read the necessary texts, the *PASSBOOK® SERIES* furnishes the one special preparation which may assure passing with confidence, instead of failing with insecurity. Examination questions – together with answers – are furnished as the basic vehicle for study so that the mysteries of the examination and its compounding difficulties may be eliminated or diminished by a sure method.

This book is meant to help you pass your examination provided that you qualify and are serious in your objective.

The entire field is reviewed through the huge store of content information which is succinctly presented through a provocative and challenging approach – the question-and-answer method.

A climate of success is established by furnishing the correct answers at the end of each test.

You soon learn to recognize types of questions, forms of questions, and patterns of questioning. You may even begin to anticipate expected outcomes.

You perceive that many questions are repeated or adapted so that you can gain acute insights, which may enable you to score many sure points.

You learn how to confront new questions, or types of questions, and to attack them confidently and work out the correct answers.

You note objectives and emphases, and recognize pitfalls and dangers, so that you may make positive educational adjustments.

Moreover, you are kept fully informed in relation to new concepts, methods, practices, and directions in the field.

You discover that you are actually taking the examination all the time: you are preparing for the examination by "taking" an examination, not by reading extraneous and/or supererogatory textbooks.

In short, this PASSBOOK®, used directedly, should be an important factor in helping you to pass your test.

TRANSPORTATION ASSISTANT

DUTIES:
Participates in research and provides support services to planning staff in all phases of transit and paratransit systems; performs related duties as required.

SUBJECT OF EXAMINATION:
The written test is designed to evaluate knowledge, skills and /or abilities in the following areas:

1. **Transportation planning and program development, including sociological, economic, design and environmental factors** - These questions test for knowledge of the concepts, design issues, terminology and proper practices utilized in the transportation planning and analysis fields, including how best to improve the quality of life, the economy and the environment through transportation planning programs and projects.
2. **Collection, analysis and presentation of data, including basic statistics** - These questions test for knowledge of the proper procedures and methods used to gather, evaluate, organize and utilize various types of technical data and information, and the fundamental concepts, terminology and computations involved in statistical analysis for transportation and transit-related planning studies.
3. **Understanding and interpreting written material** - These questions test how well you comprehend written material. You will be provided with brief reading selections and will be asked questions about the selections. All the information required to answer the questions will be presented in the selections; you will not be required to have any special knowledge relating to the subject areas of the selections.
4. **Office record keeping** - These questions test your ability to perform common office record keeping tasks. The test consists of two or more "sets" of questions, each set concerning a different problem. Typical record keeping problems might involve the organization or collation of data from several sources; scheduling; maintaining a record system using running balances; or completion of a table summarizing data using totals, subtotals, averages and percents.

HOW TO TAKE A TEST

I. YOU MUST PASS AN EXAMINATION

A. WHAT EVERY CANDIDATE SHOULD KNOW

Examination applicants often ask us for help in preparing for the written test. What can I study in advance? What kinds of questions will be asked? How will the test be given? How will the papers be graded?

As an applicant for a civil service examination, you may be wondering about some of these things. Our purpose here is to suggest effective methods of advance study and to describe civil service examinations.

Your chances for success on this examination can be increased if you know how to prepare. Those "pre-examination jitters" can be reduced if you know what to expect. You can even experience an adventure in good citizenship if you know why civil service exams are given.

B. WHY ARE CIVIL SERVICE EXAMINATIONS GIVEN?

Civil service examinations are important to you in two ways. As a citizen, you want public jobs filled by employees who know how to do their work. As a job seeker, you want a fair chance to compete for that job on an equal footing with other candidates. The best-known means of accomplishing this two-fold goal is the competitive examination.

Exams are widely publicized throughout the nation. They may be administered for jobs in federal, state, city, municipal, town or village governments or agencies.

Any citizen may apply, with some limitations, such as the age or residence of applicants. Your experience and education may be reviewed to see whether you meet the requirements for the particular examination. When these requirements exist, they are reasonable and applied consistently to all applicants. Thus, a competitive examination may cause you some uneasiness now, but it is your privilege and safeguard.

C. HOW ARE CIVIL SERVICE EXAMS DEVELOPED?

Examinations are carefully written by trained technicians who are specialists in the field known as "psychological measurement," in consultation with recognized authorities in the field of work that the test will cover. These experts recommend the subject matter areas or skills to be tested; only those knowledges or skills important to your success on the job are included. The most reliable books and source materials available are used as references. Together, the experts and technicians judge the difficulty level of the questions.

Test technicians know how to phrase questions so that the problem is clearly stated. Their ethics do not permit "trick" or "catch" questions. Questions may have been tried out on sample groups, or subjected to statistical analysis, to determine their usefulness.

Written tests are often used in combination with performance tests, ratings of training and experience, and oral interviews. All of these measures combine to form the best-known means of finding the right person for the right job.

II. HOW TO PASS THE WRITTEN TEST

A. NATURE OF THE EXAMINATION

To prepare intelligently for civil service examinations, you should know how they differ from school examinations you have taken. In school you were assigned certain definite pages to read or subjects to cover. The examination questions were quite detailed and usually emphasized memory. Civil service exams, on the other hand, try to discover your present ability to perform the duties of a position, plus your potentiality to learn these duties. In other words, a civil service exam attempts to predict how successful you will be. Questions cover such a broad area that they cannot be as minute and detailed as school exam questions.

In the public service similar kinds of work, or positions, are grouped together in one "class." This process is known as *position-classification*. All the positions in a class are paid according to the salary range for that class. One class title covers all of these positions, and they are all tested by the same examination.

B. FOUR BASIC STEPS

1) Study the announcement

How, then, can you know what subjects to study? Our best answer is: "Learn as much as possible about the class of positions for which you've applied." The exam will test the knowledge, skills and abilities needed to do the work.

Your most valuable source of information about the position you want is the official exam announcement. This announcement lists the training and experience qualifications. Check these standards and apply only if you come reasonably close to meeting them.

The brief description of the position in the examination announcement offers some clues to the subjects which will be tested. Think about the job itself. Review the duties in your mind. Can you perform them, or are there some in which you are rusty? Fill in the blank spots in your preparation.

Many jurisdictions preview the written test in the exam announcement by including a section called "Knowledge and Abilities Required," "Scope of the Examination," or some similar heading. Here you will find out specifically what fields will be tested.

2) Review your own background

Once you learn in general what the position is all about, and what you need to know to do the work, ask yourself which subjects you already know fairly well and which need improvement. You may wonder whether to concentrate on improving your strong areas or on building some background in your fields of weakness. When the announcement has specified "some knowledge" or "considerable knowledge," or has used adjectives like "beginning principles of…" or "advanced … methods," you can get a clue as to the number and difficulty of questions to be asked in any given field. More questions, and hence broader coverage, would be included for those subjects which are more important in the work. Now weigh your strengths and weaknesses against the job requirements and prepare accordingly.

3) Determine the level of the position

Another way to tell how intensively you should prepare is to understand the level of the job for which you are applying. Is it the entering level? In other words, is this the position in which beginners in a field of work are hired? Or is it an intermediate or advanced level? Sometimes this is indicated by such words as "Junior" or "Senior" in the class title. Other jurisdictions use Roman numerals to designate the level – Clerk I, Clerk II, for example. The word "Supervisor" sometimes appears in the title. If the level is not indicated by the title, check the description of duties. Will you be working under very close supervision, or will you have responsibility for independent decisions in this work?

4) Choose appropriate study materials

Now that you know the subjects to be examined and the relative amount of each subject to be covered, you can choose suitable study materials. For beginning level jobs, or even advanced ones, if you have a pronounced weakness in some aspect of your training, read a modern, standard textbook in that field. Be sure it is up to date and has general coverage. Such books are normally available at your library, and the librarian will be glad to help you locate one. For entry-level positions, questions of appropriate difficulty are chosen – neither highly advanced questions, nor those too simple. Such questions require careful thought but not advanced training.

If the position for which you are applying is technical or advanced, you will read more advanced, specialized material. If you are already familiar with the basic principles of your field, elementary textbooks would waste your time. Concentrate on advanced textbooks and technical periodicals. Think through the concepts and review difficult problems in your field.

These are all general sources. You can get more ideas on your own initiative, following these leads. For example, training manuals and publications of the government agency which employs workers in your field can be useful, particularly for technical and professional positions. A letter or visit to the government department involved may result in more specific study suggestions, and certainly will provide you with a more definite idea of the exact nature of the position you are seeking.

III. KINDS OF TESTS

Tests are used for purposes other than measuring knowledge and ability to perform specified duties. For some positions, it is equally important to test ability to make adjustments to new situations or to profit from training. In others, basic mental abilities not dependent on information are essential. Questions which test these things may not appear as pertinent to the duties of the position as those which test for knowledge and information. Yet they are often highly important parts of a fair examination. For very general questions, it is almost impossible to help you direct your study efforts. What we can do is to point out some of the more common of these general abilities needed in public service positions and describe some typical questions.

1) General information

Broad, general information has been found useful for predicting job success in some kinds of work. This is tested in a variety of ways, from vocabulary lists to questions about current events. Basic background in some field of work, such as sociology or economics, may be sampled in a group of questions. Often these are principles which have become familiar to most persons through exposure rather than through formal training. It is difficult to advise you how to study for these questions; being alert to the world around you is our best suggestion.

2) Verbal ability

An example of an ability needed in many positions is verbal or language ability. Verbal ability is, in brief, the ability to use and understand words. Vocabulary and grammar tests are typical measures of this ability. Reading comprehension or paragraph interpretation questions are common in many kinds of civil service tests. You are given a paragraph of written material and asked to find its central meaning.

3) Numerical ability

Number skills can be tested by the familiar arithmetic problem, by checking paired lists of numbers to see which are alike and which are different, or by interpreting charts and graphs. In the latter test, a graph may be printed in the test booklet which you are asked to use as the basis for answering questions.

4) Observation

A popular test for law-enforcement positions is the observation test. A picture is shown to you for several minutes, then taken away. Questions about the picture test your ability to observe both details and larger elements.

5) Following directions

In many positions in the public service, the employee must be able to carry out written instructions dependably and accurately. You may be given a chart with several columns, each column listing a variety of information. The questions require you to carry out directions involving the information given in the chart.

6) Skills and aptitudes

Performance tests effectively measure some manual skills and aptitudes. When the skill is one in which you are trained, such as typing or shorthand, you can practice. These tests are often very much like those given in business school or high school courses. For many of the other skills and aptitudes, however, no short-time preparation can be made. Skills and abilities natural to you or that you have developed throughout your lifetime are being tested.

Many of the general questions just described provide all the data needed to answer the questions and ask you to use your reasoning ability to find the answers. Your best preparation for these tests, as well as for tests of facts and ideas, is to be at your physical and mental best. You, no doubt, have your own methods of getting into an exam-taking mood and keeping "in shape." The next section lists some ideas on this subject.

IV. KINDS OF QUESTIONS

Only rarely is the "essay" question, which you answer in narrative form, used in civil service tests. Civil service tests are usually of the short-answer type. Full instructions for answering these questions will be given to you at the examination. But in case this is your first experience with short-answer questions and separate answer sheets, here is what you need to know:

1) Multiple-choice Questions

Most popular of the short-answer questions is the "multiple choice" or "best answer" question. It can be used, for example, to test for factual knowledge, ability to solve problems or judgment in meeting situations found at work.

A multiple-choice question is normally one of three types—
- It can begin with an incomplete statement followed by several possible endings. You are to find the one ending which *best* completes the statement, although some of the others may not be entirely wrong.
- It can also be a complete statement in the form of a question which is answered by choosing one of the statements listed.

- It can be in the form of a problem – again you select the best answer.

Here is an example of a multiple-choice question with a discussion which should give you some clues as to the method for choosing the right answer:

When an employee has a complaint about his assignment, the action which will *best* help him overcome his difficulty is to
- A. discuss his difficulty with his coworkers
- B. take the problem to the head of the organization
- C. take the problem to the person who gave him the assignment
- D. say nothing to anyone about his complaint

In answering this question, you should study each of the choices to find which is best. Consider choice "A" – Certainly an employee may discuss his complaint with fellow employees, but no change or improvement can result, and the complaint remains unresolved. Choice "B" is a poor choice since the head of the organization probably does not know what assignment you have been given, and taking your problem to him is known as "going over the head" of the supervisor. The supervisor, or person who made the assignment, is the person who can clarify it or correct any injustice. Choice "C" is, therefore, correct. To say nothing, as in choice "D," is unwise. Supervisors have and interest in knowing the problems employees are facing, and the employee is seeking a solution to his problem.

2) True/False Questions

The "true/false" or "right/wrong" form of question is sometimes used. Here a complete statement is given. Your job is to decide whether the statement is right or wrong.

SAMPLE: A roaming cell-phone call to a nearby city costs less than a non-roaming call to a distant city.

This statement is wrong, or false, since roaming calls are more expensive.

This is not a complete list of all possible question forms, although most of the others are variations of these common types. You will always get complete directions for answering questions. Be sure you understand *how* to mark your answers – ask questions until you do.

V. RECORDING YOUR ANSWERS

Computer terminals are used more and more today for many different kinds of exams.

For an examination with very few applicants, you may be told to record your answers in the test booklet itself. Separate answer sheets are much more common. If this separate answer sheet is to be scored by machine – and this is often the case – it is highly important that you mark your answers correctly in order to get credit.

An electronic scoring machine is often used in civil service offices because of the speed with which papers can be scored. Machine-scored answer sheets must be marked with a pencil, which will be given to you. This pencil has a high graphite content which responds to the electronic scoring machine. As a matter of fact, stray dots may register as answers, so do not let your pencil rest on the answer sheet while you are pondering the correct answer. Also, if your pencil lead breaks or is otherwise defective, ask for another.

Since the answer sheet will be dropped in a slot in the scoring machine, be careful not to bend the corners or get the paper crumpled.

The answer sheet normally has five vertical columns of numbers, with 30 numbers to a column. These numbers correspond to the question numbers in your test booklet. After each number, going across the page are four or five pairs of dotted lines. These short dotted lines have small letters or numbers above them. The first two pairs may also have a "T" or "F" above the letters. This indicates that the first two pairs only are to be used if the questions are of the true-false type. If the questions are multiple choice, disregard the "T" and "F" and pay attention only to the small letters or numbers.

Answer your questions in the manner of the sample that follows:

32. The largest city in the United States is
    A. Washington, D.C.
    B. New York City
    C. Chicago
    D. Detroit
    E. San Francisco

1) Choose the answer you think is best. (New York City is the largest, so "B" is correct.)
2) Find the row of dotted lines numbered the same as the question you are answering. (Find row number 32)
3) Find the pair of dotted lines corresponding to the answer. (Find the pair of lines under the mark "B.")
4) Make a solid black mark between the dotted lines.

VI. BEFORE THE TEST

Common sense will help you find procedures to follow to get ready for an examination. Too many of us, however, overlook these sensible measures. Indeed, nervousness and fatigue have been found to be the most serious reasons why applicants fail to do their best on civil service tests. Here is a list of reminders:

- Begin your preparation early – Don't wait until the last minute to go scurrying around for books and materials or to find out what the position is all about.
- Prepare continuously – An hour a night for a week is better than an all-night cram session. This has been definitely established. What is more, a night a week for a month will return better dividends than crowding your study into a shorter period of time.
- Locate the place of the exam – You have been sent a notice telling you when and where to report for the examination. If the location is in a different town or otherwise unfamiliar to you, it would be well to inquire the best route and learn something about the building.
- Relax the night before the test – Allow your mind to rest. Do not study at all that night. Plan some mild recreation or diversion; then go to bed early and get a good night's sleep.
- Get up early enough to make a leisurely trip to the place for the test – This way unforeseen events, traffic snarls, unfamiliar buildings, etc. will not upset you.
- Dress comfortably – A written test is not a fashion show. You will be known by number and not by name, so wear something comfortable.

- Leave excess paraphernalia at home – Shopping bags and odd bundles will get in your way. You need bring only the items mentioned in the official notice you received; usually everything you need is provided. Do not bring reference books to the exam. They will only confuse those last minutes and be taken away from you when in the test room.
- Arrive somewhat ahead of time – If because of transportation schedules you must get there very early, bring a newspaper or magazine to take your mind off yourself while waiting.
- Locate the examination room – When you have found the proper room, you will be directed to the seat or part of the room where you will sit. Sometimes you are given a sheet of instructions to read while you are waiting. Do not fill out any forms until you are told to do so; just read them and be prepared.
- Relax and prepare to listen to the instructions
- If you have any physical problem that may keep you from doing your best, be sure to tell the test administrator. If you are sick or in poor health, you really cannot do your best on the exam. You can come back and take the test some other time.

VII. AT THE TEST

The day of the test is here and you have the test booklet in your hand. The temptation to get going is very strong. Caution! There is more to success than knowing the right answers. You must know how to identify your papers and understand variations in the type of short-answer question used in this particular examination. Follow these suggestions for maximum results from your efforts:

1) Cooperate with the monitor

The test administrator has a duty to create a situation in which you can be as much at ease as possible. He will give instructions, tell you when to begin, check to see that you are marking your answer sheet correctly, and so on. He is not there to guard you, although he will see that your competitors do not take unfair advantage. He wants to help you do your best.

2) Listen to all instructions

Don't jump the gun! Wait until you understand all directions. In most civil service tests you get more time than you need to answer the questions. So don't be in a hurry. Read each word of instructions until you clearly understand the meaning. Study the examples, listen to all announcements and follow directions. Ask questions if you do not understand what to do.

3) Identify your papers

Civil service exams are usually identified by number only. You will be assigned a number; you must not put your name on your test papers. Be sure to copy your number correctly. Since more than one exam may be given, copy your exact examination title.

4) Plan your time

Unless you are told that a test is a "speed" or "rate of work" test, speed itself is usually not important. Time enough to answer all the questions will be provided, but this does not mean that you have all day. An overall time limit has been set. Divide the total time (in minutes) by the number of questions to determine the approximate time you have for each question.

5) Do not linger over difficult questions

If you come across a difficult question, mark it with a paper clip (useful to have along) and come back to it when you have been through the booklet. One caution if you do this – be sure to skip a number on your answer sheet as well. Check often to be sure that you have not lost your place and that you are marking in the row numbered the same as the question you are answering.

6) Read the questions

Be sure you know what the question asks! Many capable people are unsuccessful because they failed to *read* the questions correctly.

7) Answer all questions

Unless you have been instructed that a penalty will be deducted for incorrect answers, it is better to guess than to omit a question.

8) Speed tests

It is often better NOT to guess on speed tests. It has been found that on timed tests people are tempted to spend the last few seconds before time is called in marking answers at random – without even reading them – in the hope of picking up a few extra points. To discourage this practice, the instructions may warn you that your score will be "corrected" for guessing. That is, a penalty will be applied. The incorrect answers will be deducted from the correct ones, or some other penalty formula will be used.

9) Review your answers

If you finish before time is called, go back to the questions you guessed or omitted to give them further thought. Review other answers if you have time.

10) Return your test materials

If you are ready to leave before others have finished or time is called, take ALL your materials to the monitor and leave quietly. Never take any test material with you. The monitor can discover whose papers are not complete, and taking a test booklet may be grounds for disqualification.

VIII. EXAMINATION TECHNIQUES

1) Read the general instructions carefully. These are usually printed on the first page of the exam booklet. As a rule, these instructions refer to the timing of the examination; the fact that you should not start work until the signal and must stop work at a signal, etc. If there are any *special* instructions, such as a choice of questions to be answered, make sure that you note this instruction carefully.

2) When you are ready to start work on the examination, that is as soon as the signal has been given, read the instructions to each question booklet, underline any key words or phrases, such as *least, best, outline, describe* and the like. In this way you will tend to answer as requested rather than discover on reviewing your paper that you *listed without describing*, that you selected the *worst* choice rather than the *best* choice, etc.

3) If the examination is of the objective or multiple-choice type – that is, each question will also give a series of possible answers: A, B, C or D, and you are called upon to select the best answer and write the letter next to that answer on your answer paper – it is advisable to start answering each question in turn. There may be anywhere from 50 to 100 such questions in the three or four hours allotted and you can see how much time would be taken if you read through all the questions before beginning to answer any. Furthermore, if you come across a question or group of questions which you know would be difficult to answer, it would undoubtedly affect your handling of all the other questions.

4) If the examination is of the essay type and contains but a few questions, it is a moot point as to whether you should read all the questions before starting to answer any one. Of course, if you are given a choice – say five out of seven and the like – then it is essential to read all the questions so you can eliminate the two that are most difficult. If, however, you are asked to answer all the questions, there may be danger in trying to answer the easiest one first because you may find that you will spend too much time on it. The best technique is to answer the first question, then proceed to the second, etc.

5) Time your answers. Before the exam begins, write down the time it started, then add the time allowed for the examination and write down the time it must be completed, then divide the time available somewhat as follows:
    - If 3-1/2 hours are allowed, that would be 210 minutes. If you have 80 objective-type questions, that would be an average of 2-1/2 minutes per question. Allow yourself no more than 2 minutes per question, or a total of 160 minutes, which will permit about 50 minutes to review.
    - If for the time allotment of 210 minutes there are 7 essay questions to answer, that would average about 30 minutes a question. Give yourself only 25 minutes per question so that you have about 35 minutes to review.

6) The most important instruction is to *read each question* and make sure you know what is wanted. The second most important instruction is to *time yourself properly* so that you answer every question. The third most important instruction is to *answer every question*. Guess if you have to but include something for each question. Remember that you will receive no credit for a blank and will probably receive some credit if you write something in answer to an essay question. If you guess a letter – say "B" for a multiple-choice question – you may have guessed right. If you leave a blank as an answer to a multiple-choice question, the examiners may respect your feelings but it will not add a point to your score. Some exams may penalize you for wrong answers, so in such cases *only*, you may not want to guess unless you have some basis for your answer.

7) Suggestions
    a. Objective-type questions
        1. Examine the question booklet for proper sequence of pages and questions
        2. Read all instructions carefully
        3. Skip any question which seems too difficult; return to it after all other questions have been answered
        4. Apportion your time properly; do not spend too much time on any single question or group of questions

5. Note and underline key words – *all, most, fewest, least, best, worst, same, opposite,* etc.
6. Pay particular attention to negatives
7. Note unusual option, e.g., unduly long, short, complex, different or similar in content to the body of the question
8. Observe the use of "hedging" words – *probably, may, most likely,* etc.
9. Make sure that your answer is put next to the same number as the question
10. Do not second-guess unless you have good reason to believe the second answer is definitely more correct
11. Cross out original answer if you decide another answer is more accurate; do not erase until you are ready to hand your paper in
12. Answer all questions; guess unless instructed otherwise
13. Leave time for review

b. Essay questions
1. Read each question carefully
2. Determine exactly what is wanted. Underline key words or phrases.
3. Decide on outline or paragraph answer
4. Include many different points and elements unless asked to develop any one or two points or elements
5. Show impartiality by giving pros and cons unless directed to select one side only
6. Make and write down any assumptions you find necessary to answer the questions
7. Watch your English, grammar, punctuation and choice of words
8. Time your answers; don't crowd material

8) Answering the essay question

Most essay questions can be answered by framing the specific response around several key words or ideas. Here are a few such key words or ideas:

M's: manpower, materials, methods, money, management
P's: purpose, program, policy, plan, procedure, practice, problems, pitfalls, personnel, public relations

a. Six basic steps in handling problems:
1. Preliminary plan and background development
2. Collect information, data and facts
3. Analyze and interpret information, data and facts
4. Analyze and develop solutions as well as make recommendations
5. Prepare report and sell recommendations
6. Install recommendations and follow up effectiveness

b. Pitfalls to avoid
1. *Taking things for granted* – A statement of the situation does not necessarily imply that each of the elements is necessarily true; for example, a complaint may be invalid and biased so that all that can be taken for granted is that a complaint has been registered

2. *Considering only one side of a situation* – Wherever possible, indicate several alternatives and then point out the reasons you selected the best one
3. *Failing to indicate follow up* – Whenever your answer indicates action on your part, make certain that you will take proper follow-up action to see how successful your recommendations, procedures or actions turn out to be
4. *Taking too long in answering any single question* – Remember to time your answers properly

IX. AFTER THE TEST

Scoring procedures differ in detail among civil service jurisdictions although the general principles are the same. Whether the papers are hand-scored or graded by machine we have described, they are nearly always graded by number. That is, the person who marks the paper knows only the number – never the name – of the applicant. Not until all the papers have been graded will they be matched with names. If other tests, such as training and experience or oral interview ratings have been given, scores will be combined. Different parts of the examination usually have different weights. For example, the written test might count 60 percent of the final grade, and a rating of training and experience 40 percent. In many jurisdictions, veterans will have a certain number of points added to their grades.

After the final grade has been determined, the names are placed in grade order and an eligible list is established. There are various methods for resolving ties between those who get the same final grade – probably the most common is to place first the name of the person whose application was received first. Job offers are made from the eligible list in the order the names appear on it. You will be notified of your grade and your rank as soon as all these computations have been made. This will be done as rapidly as possible.

People who are found to meet the requirements in the announcement are called "eligibles." Their names are put on a list of eligible candidates. An eligible's chances of getting a job depend on how high he stands on this list and how fast agencies are filling jobs from the list.

When a job is to be filled from a list of eligibles, the agency asks for the names of people on the list of eligibles for that job. When the civil service commission receives this request, it sends to the agency the names of the three people highest on this list. Or, if the job to be filled has specialized requirements, the office sends the agency the names of the top three persons who meet these requirements from the general list.

The appointing officer makes a choice from among the three people whose names were sent to him. If the selected person accepts the appointment, the names of the others are put back on the list to be considered for future openings.

That is the rule in hiring from all kinds of eligible lists, whether they are for typist, carpenter, chemist, or something else. For every vacancy, the appointing officer has his choice of any one of the top three eligibles on the list. This explains why the person whose name is on top of the list sometimes does not get an appointment when some of the persons lower on the list do. If the appointing officer chooses the second or third eligible, the No. 1 eligible does not get a job at once, but stays on the list until he is appointed or the list is terminated.

X. HOW TO PASS THE INTERVIEW TEST

The examination for which you applied requires an oral interview test. You have already taken the written test and you are now being called for the interview test – the final part of the formal examination.

You may think that it is not possible to prepare for an interview test and that there are no procedures to follow during an interview. Our purpose is to point out some things you can do in advance that will help you and some good rules to follow and pitfalls to avoid while you are being interviewed.

What is an interview supposed to test?

The written examination is designed to test the technical knowledge and competence of the candidate; the oral is designed to evaluate intangible qualities, not readily measured otherwise, and to establish a list showing the relative fitness of each candidate – as measured against his competitors – for the position sought. Scoring is not on the basis of "right" and "wrong," but on a sliding scale of values ranging from "not passable" to "outstanding." As a matter of fact, it is possible to achieve a relatively low score without a single "incorrect" answer because of evident weakness in the qualities being measured.

Occasionally, an examination may consist entirely of an oral test – either an individual or a group oral. In such cases, information is sought concerning the technical knowledges and abilities of the candidate, since there has been no written examination for this purpose. More commonly, however, an oral test is used to supplement a written examination.

Who conducts interviews?

The composition of oral boards varies among different jurisdictions. In nearly all, a representative of the personnel department serves as chairman. One of the members of the board may be a representative of the department in which the candidate would work. In some cases, "outside experts" are used, and, frequently, a businessman or some other representative of the general public is asked to serve. Labor and management or other special groups may be represented. The aim is to secure the services of experts in the appropriate field.

However the board is composed, it is a good idea (and not at all improper or unethical) to ascertain in advance of the interview who the members are and what groups they represent. When you are introduced to them, you will have some idea of their backgrounds and interests, and at least you will not stutter and stammer over their names.

What should be done before the interview?

While knowledge about the board members is useful and takes some of the surprise element out of the interview, there is other preparation which is more substantive. It *is* possible to prepare for an oral interview – in several ways:

1) Keep a copy of your application and review it carefully before the interview

This may be the only document before the oral board, and the starting point of the interview. Know what education and experience you have listed there, and the sequence and dates of all of it. Sometimes the board will ask you to review the highlights of your experience for them; you should not have to hem and haw doing it.

2) Study the class specification and the examination announcement

Usually, the oral board has one or both of these to guide them. The qualities, characteristics or knowledges required by the position sought are stated in these documents. They offer valuable clues as to the nature of the oral interview. For example, if the job involves supervisory responsibilities, the announcement will usually indicate that knowledge of modern supervisory methods and the qualifications of the candidate as a supervisor will be tested. If so, you can expect such questions, frequently in the form of a hypothetical situation which you are expected to solve. NEVER go into an oral without knowledge of the duties and responsibilities of the job you seek.

3) Think through each qualification required

Try to visualize the kind of questions you would ask if you were a board member. How well could you answer them? Try especially to appraise your own knowledge and background in each area, *measured against the job sought*, and identify any areas in which you are weak. Be critical and realistic – do not flatter yourself.

4) Do some general reading in areas in which you feel you may be weak

For example, if the job involves supervision and your past experience has NOT, some general reading in supervisory methods and practices, particularly in the field of human relations, might be useful. Do NOT study agency procedures or detailed manuals. The oral board will be testing your understanding and capacity, not your memory.

5) Get a good night's sleep and watch your general health and mental attitude

You will want a clear head at the interview. Take care of a cold or any other minor ailment, and of course, no hangovers.

What should be done on the day of the interview?

Now comes the day of the interview itself. Give yourself plenty of time to get there. Plan to arrive somewhat ahead of the scheduled time, particularly if your appointment is in the fore part of the day. If a previous candidate fails to appear, the board might be ready for you a bit early. By early afternoon an oral board is almost invariably behind schedule if there are many candidates, and you may have to wait. Take along a book or magazine to read, or your application to review, but leave any extraneous material in the waiting room when you go in for your interview. In any event, relax and compose yourself.

The matter of dress is important. The board is forming impressions about you – from your experience, your manners, your attitude, and your appearance. Give your personal appearance careful attention. Dress your best, but not your flashiest. Choose conservative, appropriate clothing, and be sure it is immaculate. This is a business interview, and your appearance should indicate that you regard it as such. Besides, being well groomed and properly dressed will help boost your confidence.

Sooner or later, someone will call your name and escort you into the interview room. *This is it.* From here on you are on your own. It is too late for any more preparation. But remember, you asked for this opportunity to prove your fitness, and you are here because your request was granted.

What happens when you go in?

The usual sequence of events will be as follows: The clerk (who is often the board stenographer) will introduce you to the chairman of the oral board, who will introduce you to the other members of the board. Acknowledge the introductions before you sit down. Do not be surprised if you find a microphone facing you or a stenotypist sitting by. Oral interviews are usually recorded in the event of an appeal or other review.

Usually the chairman of the board will open the interview by reviewing the highlights of your education and work experience from your application – primarily for the benefit of the other members of the board, as well as to get the material into the record. Do not interrupt or comment unless there is an error or significant misinterpretation; if that is the case, do not hesitate. But do not quibble about insignificant matters. Also, he will usually ask you some question about your education, experience or your present job – partly to get you to start talking and to establish the interviewing "rapport." He may start the actual questioning, or turn it over to one of the other members. Frequently, each member undertakes the questioning on a particular area, one in which he is perhaps most competent, so you can expect each member to participate in the examination. Because time is limited, you may also expect some rather abrupt switches in the direction the questioning takes, so do not be upset by it. Normally, a board member will not pursue a single line of questioning unless he discovers a particular strength or weakness.

After each member has participated, the chairman will usually ask whether any member has any further questions, then will ask you if you have anything you wish to add. Unless you are expecting this question, it may floor you. Worse, it may start you off on an extended, extemporaneous speech. The board is not usually seeking more information. The question is principally to offer you a last opportunity to present further qualifications or to indicate that you have nothing to add. So, if you feel that a significant qualification or characteristic has been overlooked, it is proper to point it out in a sentence or so. Do not compliment the board on the thoroughness of their examination – they have been sketchy, and you know it. If you wish, merely say, "No thank you, I have nothing further to add." This is a point where you can "talk yourself out" of a good impression or fail to present an important bit of information. Remember, *you close the interview yourself*.

The chairman will then say, "That is all, Mr. _____, thank you." Do not be startled; the interview is over, and quicker than you think. Thank him, gather your belongings and take your leave. Save your sigh of relief for the other side of the door.

How to put your best foot forward

Throughout this entire process, you may feel that the board individually and collectively is trying to pierce your defenses, seek out your hidden weaknesses and embarrass and confuse you. Actually, this is not true. They are obliged to make an appraisal of your qualifications for the job you are seeking, and they want to see you in your best light. Remember, they must interview all candidates and a non-cooperative candidate may become a failure in spite of their best efforts to bring out his qualifications. Here are 15 suggestions that will help you:

1) Be natural – Keep your attitude confident, not cocky

If you are not confident that you can do the job, do not expect the board to be. Do not apologize for your weaknesses, try to bring out your strong points. The board is interested in a positive, not negative, presentation. Cockiness will antagonize any board member and make him wonder if you are covering up a weakness by a false show of strength.

2) Get comfortable, but don't lounge or sprawl

Sit erectly but not stiffly. A careless posture may lead the board to conclude that you are careless in other things, or at least that you are not impressed by the importance of the occasion. Either conclusion is natural, even if incorrect. Do not fuss with your clothing, a pencil or an ashtray. Your hands may occasionally be useful to emphasize a point; do not let them become a point of distraction.

3) Do not wisecrack or make small talk

This is a serious situation, and your attitude should show that you consider it as such. Further, the time of the board is limited – they do not want to waste it, and neither should you.

4) Do not exaggerate your experience or abilities
In the first place, from information in the application or other interviews and sources, the board may know more about you than you think. Secondly, you probably will not get away with it. An experienced board is rather adept at spotting such a situation, so do not take the chance.

5) If you know a board member, do not make a point of it, yet do not hide it
Certainly you are not fooling him, and probably not the other members of the board. Do not try to take advantage of your acquaintanceship – it will probably do you little good.

6) Do not dominate the interview
Let the board do that. They will give you the clues – do not assume that you have to do all the talking. Realize that the board has a number of questions to ask you, and do not try to take up all the interview time by showing off your extensive knowledge of the answer to the first one.

7) Be attentive
You only have 20 minutes or so, and you should keep your attention at its sharpest throughout. When a member is addressing a problem or question to you, give him your undivided attention. Address your reply principally to him, but do not exclude the other board members.

8) Do not interrupt
A board member may be stating a problem for you to analyze. He will ask you a question when the time comes. Let him state the problem, and wait for the question.

9) Make sure you understand the question
Do not try to answer until you are sure what the question is. If it is not clear, restate it in your own words or ask the board member to clarify it for you. However, do not haggle about minor elements.

10) Reply promptly but not hastily
A common entry on oral board rating sheets is "candidate responded readily," or "candidate hesitated in replies." Respond as promptly and quickly as you can, but do not jump to a hasty, ill-considered answer.

11) Do not be peremptory in your answers
A brief answer is proper – but do not fire your answer back. That is a losing game from your point of view. The board member can probably ask questions much faster than you can answer them.

12) Do not try to create the answer you think the board member wants
He is interested in what kind of mind you have and how it works – not in playing games. Furthermore, he can usually spot this practice and will actually grade you down on it.

13) Do not switch sides in your reply merely to agree with a board member
Frequently, a member will take a contrary position merely to draw you out and to see if you are willing and able to defend your point of view. Do not start a debate, yet do not surrender a good position. If a position is worth taking, it is worth defending.

14) Do not be afraid to admit an error in judgment if you are shown to be wrong

The board knows that you are forced to reply without any opportunity for careful consideration. Your answer may be demonstrably wrong. If so, admit it and get on with the interview.

15) Do not dwell at length on your present job

The opening question may relate to your present assignment. Answer the question but do not go into an extended discussion. You are being examined for a *new* job, not your present one. As a matter of fact, try to phrase ALL your answers in terms of the job for which you are being examined.

Basis of Rating

Probably you will forget most of these "do's" and "don'ts" when you walk into the oral interview room. Even remembering them all will not ensure you a passing grade. Perhaps you did not have the qualifications in the first place. But remembering them will help you to put your best foot forward, without treading on the toes of the board members.

Rumor and popular opinion to the contrary notwithstanding, an oral board wants you to make the best appearance possible. They know you are under pressure – but they also want to see how you respond to it as a guide to what your reaction would be under the pressures of the job you seek. They will be influenced by the degree of poise you display, the personal traits you show and the manner in which you respond.

ABOUT THIS BOOK

This book contains tests divided into Examination Sections. Go through each test, answering every question in the margin. We have also attached a sample answer sheet at the back of the book that can be removed and used. At the end of each test look at the answer key and check your answers. On the ones you got wrong, look at the right answer choice and learn. Do not fill in the answers first. Do not memorize the questions and answers, but understand the answer and principles involved. On your test, the questions will likely be different from the samples. Questions are changed and new ones added. If you understand these past questions you should have success with any changes that arise. Tests may consist of several types of questions. We have additional books on each subject should more study be advisable or necessary for you. Finally, the more you study, the better prepared you will be. This book is intended to be the last thing you study before you walk into the examination room. Prior study of relevant texts is also recommended. NLC publishes some of these in our Fundamental Series. Knowledge and good sense are important factors in passing your exam. Good luck also helps. So now study this Passbook, absorb the material contained within and take that knowledge into the examination. Then do your best to pass that exam.

EXAMINATION SECTION

EXAMINATION SECTION
TEST 1

DIRECTIONS: Each question or incomplete statement is followed by several suggested answers or completions. Select the one that Best answers the question or completes the statement. *PRINT THE LETTER OF THE CORRECT ANSWER IN THE SPACE AT THE RIGHT.*

Questions 1-4.

DIRECTIONS: Answer Questions 1 to 4 based on the information given in the traffic volume table below.

TRAFFIC VOLUME COUNTS

Time (A.M.)	Main Street Northbound	Main Street Southbound	Cross Street Eastbound	Cross Street Westbound
7:00- 7:15	100	100	70	60
7:15- 7:30	110	100	80	70
7:30- 7:45	150	140	110	100
7:45- 8:00	170	160	140	130
8:00- 8:15	210	190	120	110
8:15- 8:30	180	170	90	80
8:30- 8:45	160	140	70	60
8:45- 9:00	150	160	70	50
9:00- 9:15	140	150	50	50
9:15- 9:30	130	120	40	20
9:30- 9:45	120	110	30	30
9:45-10:00	120	100	30	30

1. The hour during which traffic, moving in both directions on Main Street, reached its *peak* was

   A. 7:30 - 8:30
   B. 7:45 - 8:45
   C. 8:00 - 9:00
   D. 8:15 - 9:15

2. The hour during which traffic volume, moving in both directions on Cross Street, reached its *peak* was

   A. 7:30 - 8:30
   B. 7:45 - 8:45
   C. 8:00 - 9:00
   D. 8:15 - 9:15

3. The HIGHEST average hourly volume over the three-hour period 7:00 to 10:00 was recorded for

   A. Main Street northbound
   B. Main Street southbound
   C. Cross Street eastbound
   D. Cross Street westbound

4. The *peak* 15-minute traffic volume for all directions of travel occurred between

   A. 7:30 - 7:45
   B. 7:45 - 8:00
   C. 8:00 - 8:15
   D. 8:15 - 8:30

5. Which of the following statements relating to one-way streets is CORRECT?
   One-way streets

1

A. increase turning movement conflicts between vehicles
B. decrease street capacity
C. decrease accident hazards for pedestrians
D. make it impossible to time traffic signals to control speeds

Questions 6-11.

DIRECTIONS: Answer Questions 6 to 11 based on the information given in Figure 1 below.

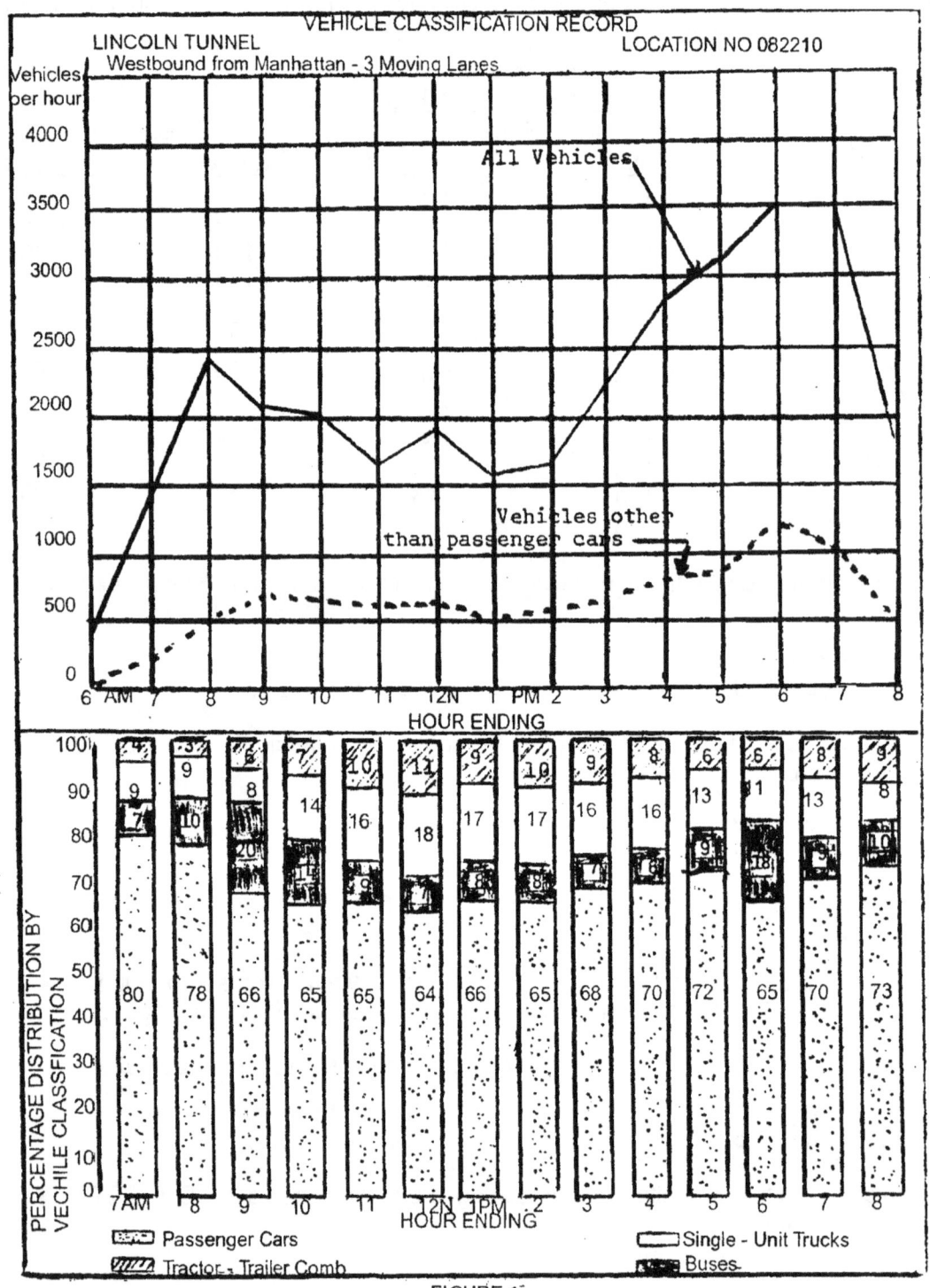

FIGURE 1

6. The total number of all vehicles traveling through the Lincoln Tunnel westbound from Manhattan between the hours of 6 A.M. and 12 Noon is *most nearly*

    A. 5,500   B. 7,500   C. 9,500   D. 11,500

7. The number of passenger cars recorded during the hour ending at 7 P.M. was *most nearly*

    A. 235   B. 1160   C. 2450   D. 3500

8. Excluding passenger cars, the AVERAGE number of vehicles per moving lane recorded during the peak hour was *most nearly*

    A. 420   B. 1180   C. 1250   D. 3550

9. The percentage of buses recorded between 6 A.M. and 8 P.M. ranged between

    A. 3% and 11%
    B. 8% and 18%
    C. 6% and 20%
    D. 64% and 80%

10. During the study period, the percentage of single unit trucks *exceeded* the percentage of buses for _____ hours.

    A. 4   B. 5   C. 9   D. 10

11. For all vehicles recorded, the recorded traffic volume during the morning peak hour was *most nearly* _____ of the volume during the evening peak hour.

    A. 40%   B. 50%   C. 60%   D. 70%

12. In urban areas, traffic volume is usually LOWEST during the month of

    A. January   B. March   C. August   D. October

13. In urban shopping areas, the *peak* traffic activity USUALLY occurs during

    A. Monday afternoon and Friday night
    B. Friday night and Saturday afternoon
    C. Thursday night and Saturday afternoon
    D. Monday night and Friday night

14. In the metric system, the unit that is closest to a mile is a

    A. centimeter
    B. liter
    C. millimeter
    D. kilometer

Questions 15-16.

DIRECTIONS: Questions 15 and 16 refer to the diagram at the top of the following Page 4.

15. Vehicle X in the diagram is heading in which direction?

    A. Southeast
    B. Southwest
    C. Northeast
    D. Northwest

16. If Vehicle X in the diagram makes a right turn at the intersection, it will be headed

    A. southeast
    B. southwest
    C. northeast
    D. northwest

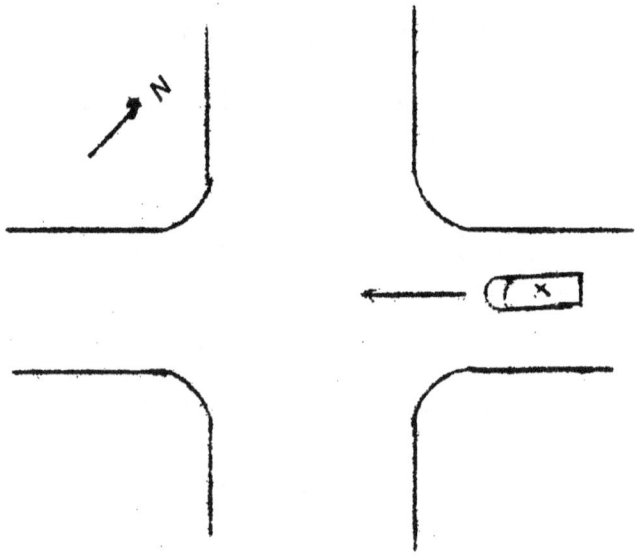

17. The one of the following that is NOT a function of channelization is 17.____

    A. control the angle of conflict
    B. favor certain turning movements
    C. protect pedestrians
    D. increase the pavement area within an intersection

18. The time of display of the yellow signal indication following the green signal indication is called the 18.____

    A. clearance interval B. time cycle
    C. traffic phase   D. interval sequence

19. A lane constructed for the purpose of allowing vehicles entering a highway to increase speed to a rate that is safe for merging with through traffic is called a(n) _____ lane. 19.____

    A. auxiliary   B. through
    C. acceleration   D. deceleration

20. A traffic volume count which records the number and types of vehicles passing a given point is called a _____ count. 20.____

    A. rate-of-flow   B. capacity
    C. classification D. roadway

21. On highways, the MAIN purpose served by barriers between traffic going in opposite directions is to 21.____

    A. stop cars if they get out of lane
    B. minimize the glare from oncoming cars
    C. prevent cars from overturning if they have blowouts
    D. prevent head-on accidents

22. Control count stations are USUALLY used to 22.____

    A. establish seasonal and daily traffic volume characteristics
    B. make short manual traffic counts
    C. classify traffic
    D. count traffic on weekends only

23. The MAIN purpose of off-center traffic lanes is to 23.____

    A. protect slow-moving traffic from the hazards of fast-moving traffic
    B. permit the use of special traffic control
    C. provide additional capacity in one direction of travel
    D. provide a slow-down area for disabled vehicles

24. Reserved transit lanes are used to 24.____

    A. make sure buses stop at the curb
    B. reduce bus and passenger car accidents
    C. decrease transit travel times by reducing friction between buses and other vehicles
    D. make it easier for people to get on and off buses

25. The slope or grade between points X and Y shown in the diagram below is 25.____

    A. 4%   B. 10%   C. 25%   D. 50%

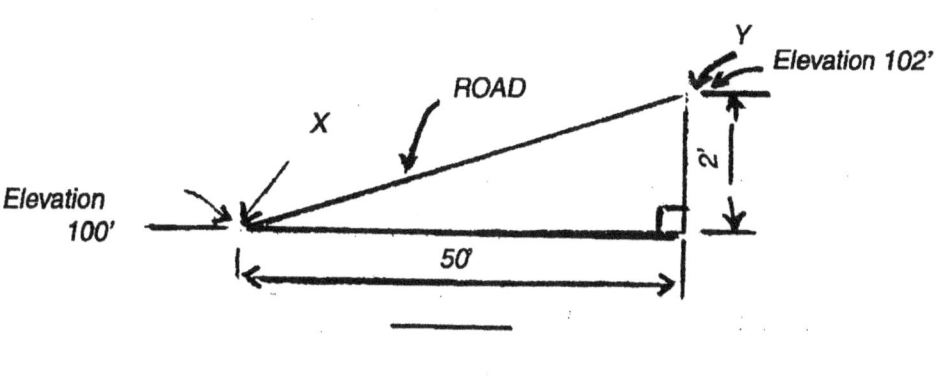

KEY (CORRECT ANSWERS)

1. B
2. A
3. A
4. C
5. C

6. D
7. C
8. A
9. C
10. C

11. D
12. A
13. B
14. D
15. B

16. D
17. D
18. A
19. C
20. C

21. D
22. A
23. C
24. C
25. A

TEST 2

DIRECTIONS: Each question or incomplete statement is followed by several suggested answers or completions. Select the one that BEST answers the question or completes the statement. *PRINT THE LETTER OF THE CORRECT ANSWER IN THE SPACE AT THE RIGHT.*

1. In the city, when parking is not otherwise restricted, commercial vehicles can park   1.____

    A. up to a maximum of one hour
    B. up to a maximum of three hours
    C. up to a maximum of eight hours
    D. without a time limitation

2. In the city, with respect to loading an parking, commercial vehicles are allowed to   2.____

    A. load or unload merchandise expeditiously in a no-standing zone
    B. park for one hour in a no-parking zone
    C. load or unload merchandise expeditiously in a no-parking zone
    D. park for one hour in a no-standing zone

3. On the Federal national highway system, highways ending in an even number run   3.____

    A. in the east-west direction
    B. both east-west or north-south
    C. in the north-south direction
    D. around cities and not through them

4. The *current* maximum allowed speed limit on Federal interstate highways is _____ miles per hour.   4.____

    A. 50   B. 55   C. 60   D. 65

5. In the city, when a vehicle is too long for a single parking meter space, the vehicle may   5.____

    A. not be parked in the parking meter area
    B. be parked using more than one space but a coin must be deposited in the meter designated for each space occupied
    C. be parked using more than one space and a coin must be deposited only in the forward parking meter
    D. be parked using more than one space and a coin must be deposited only in the rear parking meter

6. In the city, some signs indicate that stopping, standing, or parking regulations are in effect every day except Sundays. Where this sign is used, stopping, standing, or parking regulations would apply on   6.____

    A. Washington's Birthday   B. Brooklyn Day
    C. Columbus Day   D. Election Day

7. In the city, unless signs are posted indicating specific hours during which play street regulations are in effect, such regulations are in effect on designated streets FROM   7.____

    A. 7 A.M. until 4 P.M.
    B. 8 A.M. until 1/2 hour before sunset

7

C. 8 A.M. to 1/2 hour after sunset
D. 8 A.M. to 8 P.M.

8. When preparing to make a turn while driving a vehicle on a roadway, a driver should signal his intention to turn AT LEAST _____ feet in advance of the turn.

   A. 50 B. 100 C. 150 D. 200

9. Unless otherwise permitted or prohibited by posted signs, the MAXIMUM continuous period during which a vehicle may be parked on any roadway in the city is ____ hours.

   A. 8 B. 12 C. 24 D. 48

10. In the city, commercial vehicles may angle stand or angle park in

    A. any area where no parking signs are installed, provided the street is wide enough to allow the vehicle to park at an angle
    B. on any one-way street where standing is not prohibited, provided the street is wide enough to allow the vehicle to park at an angle
    C. on a two-way street in areas authorized by signs, provided that the vehicle shall not occupy more than a parking lane plus one moving lane
    D. on a two-way street in areas authorized by signs, provided that the vehicles shall not extend more than 10 feet from the curb

11. Which of the following is MOST restrictive to drivers of passenger cars?

    A. Regulations relating to parking in front of fire hydrants
    B. No parking regulations
    C. No standing regulations
    D. No stopping regulations

12. The MAXIMUM permitted speed limit in the city, unless signs indicate otherwise, is _____ mph.

    A. 25 B. 30 C. 35 D. 40

13. With regard to right-of-way at an intersection that is NOT controlled by a traffic control device, the one of the following statements that is CORRECT is

    A. the car on your right has the right-of-way
    B. the car on your left has the right-of-way
    C. a car preparing to enter the intersection has the right-of-way over a car in the intersection
    D. a car turning left has the right-of-way over a vehicle going straight ahead

14. At an intersection controlled by traffic signals, a red arrow pointing to the right means that a right turn may

    A. be made after coming to a full stop
    B. be made providing the driver yields the right-of-way to all other vehicles and pedestrians
    C. not be made during the period that the red arrow is illuminated
    D. be made only if there is another indication showing a round green signal light

15. A flashing red traffic signal has the SAME meaning as a

    A. stop sign
    B. yield sign
    C. flashing yellow traffic signal
    D. hazardous intersection warning sign

16. Traffic signals are MOST frequently installed to reduce _____ collision accidents.

    A. right-angle
    B. rear-end
    C. side-swipe
    D. head-on

17. The CORRECT color combination for warning signs is

    A. yellow lettering or symbols on a black background
    B. white lettering or symbols on a red background
    C. black lettering or symbols on a yellow background
    D. black lettering or symbols on a white background

18. A PROGRESSIVELY timed traffic signal system will

    A. turn all the signals red or green at the same time
    B. usually increase the number of rear-end accidents but reduce the number of right-angle accidents
    C. make it more hazardous for pedestrians to cross at the signalized intersections
    D. decrease the number of stops traffic is required to make

19. The EFFECT of traffic signals on accidents is that traffic signals

    A. always decrease accidents
    B. sometimes increase accidents
    C. never increase accidents
    D. have no real effect on accidents

20. With respect to traffic devices, which of the following situations should receive the LOWEST priority in terms of repair or replacement?

    A. Inoperative or malfunctioning traffic signals at an intersection
    B. Missing "No Standing - Rush Hour" regulation signs
    C. Missing "Yield" signs controlling the intersection of a minor street with a major street
    D. Inoperative parking meters along one block in a retail shopping area

21. Of the following, the BEST reason why a stop sign would be used instead of a yield sign to control traffic at an intersection is

    A. there are a larger number of rear-end accidents on the street being controlled
    B. the street being controlled is less than 36 feet wide
    C. visibility is limited at the intersection
    D. the approaches to the intersection are offset to each other

22. The USUAL color combination used on interstate signs is _____ lettering and symbols on a _____ background.

    A. white; green
    B. green; white
    C. white; black
    D. black; white

23. The geometrical shape of a railroad crossing sign is that of a(n)

    A. octagon   B. circle   C. rectangle   D. triangle

24. The STANDARD pedestrian walking speed used in timing pedestrian signals is _____ per second.

    A. 1 foot   B. 4 feet   C. 8 feet   D. 12 feet

25. A driver approaching an intersection where a sign authorizes a right turn on a red traffic signal indication may make such a turn AND

    A. has the right-of-way over all vehicles in the intersection
    B. must yield right-of-way to all vehicles and pedestrians within the intersection
    C. must yield right-of-way only to vehicles and pedestrians on the cross street
    D. has the right-of-way over other turning vehicles

KEY (CORRECT ANSWERS)

1. B		11. D	
2. C		12. B	
3. A		13. A	
4. D		14. C	
5. C		15. A	
6. B		16. A	
7. C		17. C	
8. B		18. D	
9. C		19. B	
10. C		20. D	

21. C
22. A
23. B
24. B
25. B

EXAMINATION SECTION
TEST 1

DIRECTIONS: Each question or incomplete statement is followed by several suggested answers or completions. Select the one that BEST answers the question or completes the statement. *PRINT THE LETTER OF THE CORRECT ANSWER IN THE SPACE AT THE RIGHT.*

1. The current trend among MOST ecologists is to consider the coastal zones of America   1.____

    A. a group of diverse, stable ecosystems whose respective managements require a variety of individual approaches
    B. systems that are unique to this continent and require an entirely different set of management techniques from other continental coast zones
    C. a group of unstable ecosystems whose already fragile balance has been destroyed by modern industrial practices
    D. a single natural ecosystem requiring integration of management techniques

2. Of the following methods for controlling industrial particulate discharge into the air, the one which has the GREATEST potential efficiency is   2.____

    A. wet scrubbing
    B. fabric filter bag house
    C. electrostatic precipitation
    D. cyclone filter

3. The process by which objects or solid materials are removed from a water supply is called   3.____

    A. straining   B. treatment
    C. screening   D. precipitating

4. All of the following are generally considered obstacles to United States air quality control operations EXCEPT   4.____

    A. high number of uncertain cause-effect relationships
    B. resistance from industrial operations
    C. little danger perceived by the public
    D. relatively small number of particulate contaminants that have been identified

5. The MOST critical step in any given industrial waste management program is the   5.____

    A. phase separation   B. preliminary investigation
    C. process modification   D. contaminant removal

6. The one of the following that is NOT an option for the control of coastal management offered by the Federal Coastal Management Program is   6.____

    A. direct state control
    B. local control subject to state review
    C. local control consistent with state standards
    D. regional control based upon state collaboration

7. The process through which gaseous contaminants are removed from the air is called

   A. desorption
   B. adsorption
   C. distillation
   D. precipitation

8. An automobile's catalytic converter is designed to keep all of the following contaminants from being discharged into the air EXCEPT

   A. lead
   B. carbon monoxide
   C. hydrocarbons
   D. nitrogen oxides

9. Which of the following is a chemical process of waste-water treatment?

   A. Screening
   B. Distillation
   C. Sedimentation
   D. Coagulation

10. The stage that occurs LAST in the treatment process of sanitary sewage is

    A. sedimentation
    B. screening out solids
    C. biological oxidation
    D. filtering through grit chambers

11. The element of air quality control that can be monitored but NOT managed is

    A. regulatory standards
    B. emissions
    C. meteorology and dispersion
    D. air quality

12. Currently, the rationale behind MOST water quality control operations is

    A. public health
    B. aesthetic qualities of water resource
    C. protection of aquatic life
    D. preserving recreational capabilities of water resource

13. In the process of air quality improvement, the practice used as a precleaning process before more efficient methods are applied is called

    A. electrostatic precipitation
    B. mechanical cleaning
    C. gas conditioning
    D. process modifications

14. Which of the following practiced methods for desaliniza-tion of water makes use of a salt-filtering membrane?

    A. Freezing
    B. Distillation
    C. Reverse osmosis
    D. Electrodialysis

15. The FUNDAMENTAL criterion for managing coastal basins is the

    A. geological configuration of the basin
    B. depth of the basin
    C. ecological vitality of the system
    D. degree of water exchange or flushing rate

16. The LEAST desirable method for heating gases that are intended to be released from an air cleaning unit is by

   A. direct combustion
   B. heat exchangers
   C. indirect heating of ambient air
   D. cooling entering gases

17. Of the following stages of conventional wastewater treatment, the one that occurs FIRST is

   A. chlorination	B. sedimentation
   C. oxidation	D. discharge

18. The air quality control devices capable of removing BOTH particulate and gaseous contaminants from the air are

   A. cyclone filters	B. wet scrubbers
   C. adsorbers	D. filter baghouses

19. The process of restoration is considered acceptable by MOST ecologists if it is implemented to

   A. compensate for an operation that has been projected as being harmful
   B. correct inadvertent harm or past problems
   C. mitigate the damage in advance of a harmful practice
   D. improve the aesthetics of an environment that is near development

20. Turbidity, or ultrafine particle solids in a water supply, are PRIMARILY removed through the process of

   A. screening	B. distillation
   C. coagulation	D. oxidation

21. The object of chemical removal processes in air quality control is to

   A. convert gases to particulate matter
   B. increase the water saturation point of the air medium
   C. convert gases into innocuous chemical compounds
   D. vaporize particulate matter

22. Which of the following is NOT a practice associated with the restoration of silt-polluted coastal basins?

   A. Limiting dredging to active vegetative periods
   B. Construction of bulkheads along the shore
   C. Implementation of soil conservation practices in adjacent farmlands
   D. Diversion of runoff waters from basin

23. _____ standards are applied to municipal water control operations to specify the MAXIMUM concentration of certain constituents of a given water supply.

   A. Procedural	B. Performance
   C. Investigation	D. Design

24. Which of the following is NOT among the most effective methods for the prevention of aquifer contamination?

    A. Industrial zoning
    B. Strict chemical storage rules
    C. Trenching
    D. Watershed protection

25. Of the following, the chemical process that is NOT considered a control mechanism for air quality is

    A. masking
    B. particulate conversion
    C. reduction
    D. oxidation

KEY (CORRECT ANSWERS)

1. D
2. C
3. C
4. C
5. B

6. D
7. B
8. A
9. D
10. C

11. C
12. C
13. B
14. C
15. D

16. A
17. B
18. B
19. B
20. C

21. A
22. A
23. B
24. C
25. A

TEST 2

DIRECTIONS: Each question or incomplete statement is followed by several suggested answers or completions. Select the one that BEST answers the question or completes the statement. *PRINT THE LETTER OF THE CORRECT ANSWER IN THE SPACE AT THE RIGHT.*

1. The term for the process that removes algae or turbidity from a water supply during the water treatment process is

    A. screening
    B. straining
    C. treatment
    D. discharge

    1.____

2. The method for treating groundwater contamination MOST often used for drinking water supplies is _____ treatment.

    A. chemical
    B. carbon
    C. aerobic biological
    D. ozonation/radiation

    2.____

3. Which of the following is NOT one of the primary factors determining the operation of coastal basin management?

    A. Circulation type
    B. Climate
    C. Geology
    D. Depth

    3.____

4. All of the following are practical methods for limiting the discharge of sulfur oxides into the air EXCEPT

    A. desulfurization of oil
    B. limiting coal use to low-sulfur varieties
    C. removal of sulfur from industrial water supplies
    D. removal of sulfur from coal

    4.____

5. The one of the following that is NOT a practice associated with the construction of spoil islands that will protect marina sites in coastal waters is

    A. vegetation with both upland plants and marsh grasses
    B. avoidance of existing vital areas
    C. constructing elliptical islands parallel to water flow
    D. use of fine soil materials in construction

    5.____

6. The FIRST step in any water quality control procedure is

    A. determination of the plant site
    B. compilation of data needed to reach sound decisions about objectives
    C. imposing immediate short-term controls on water quality
    D. establishment of design standards for plant operations

    6.____

7. Of the following methods for controlling industrial particulate discharge into the air, the one that makes use of gravitational forces is

    A. wet scrubbing
    B. fabric filter bag house
    C. electrostatic precipitation
    D. cyclone filter

    7.____

8. An example of a physical process of wastewater treatment is

   A. coagulation
   B. distillation
   C. ion exchange
   D. pH adjustment

9. The type of marine environment that is considered to be MOST in need of management is the

   A. lagoon
   B. bay
   C. ocean
   D. tidal river

10. Of the practiced methods for desalinization of water, the MOST widely used in the United States is

    A. freezing
    B. distillation
    C. reverse osmosis
    D. electrodialysis

11. Each of the following is a noncrystalline adsorbent used to remove contaminants from the air EXCEPT

    A. metallic oxides
    B. activated carbon
    C. silica gel
    D. D, activated alumina

12. The guiding practice of a shorelands management operation is

    A. excavating drainage canals
    B. clearing vegetation
    C. maintaining natural drainage and stream flow
    D. covering land with impervious surfaces

13. In water treatment, the mixing process during which particles form into aggregate masses that settle out is called

    A. osmosis
    B. flocculation
    C. straining
    D. oxidation

14. The type of standards applied to municipal water control operations that specify the required characteristics of a given water supply are _____ standards.

    A. design
    B. performance
    C. procedural
    D. investigation

15. _____ standards are applied to municipal water control operations that define the approaches and methods followed in water quality control activities.

    A. Procedural
    B. Design
    C. Investigation
    D. Performance

16. Marsh-grass plantings are widely used near coastal waters for all of the following purposes EXCEPT

    A. stabilizing dredge spoil
    B. creation of marshes
    C. revitalization of microorganisms
    D. creation of alternative bulkheads

17. Which of the following has NOT been widely attempted as a method for the control of automotive emissions?

    A. Reduction of automobile traffic in urban areas
    B. Altering the composition of motor fuels
    C. Filtering or converting devices for emissions
    D. Modification of the conventional engine

    17.____

18. The guiding factor for what is an acceptable MINIMUM flow into coastal ecosystems is the

    A. sedimentation of inlet basin
    B. strength of tidal backflow
    C. critical survival point for microorganisms
    D. dry-season low flows under natural conditions

    18.____

19. In preparing water that is to be considered drinkable, the PRIMARY method for odor prevention is

    A. chlorine-ammonia treatment
    B. fluoridation
    C. flocculation
    D. filtration

    19.____

20. The MOST effective method for containing a contaminant leakage plume that has deeply penetrated an underground water source is

    A. trenching
    B. installing a clay barrier
    C. well pumping
    D. chemical or biological treatment

    20.____

21. The ULTIMATE goal of the 1972 Amendment to the Water Pollution Control Act was

    A. enforceable standards limiting industrial waste disposal practices in United States waters
    B. total elimination of the discharge of pollutants into navigable United States waters
    C. banning of the production and marketing of harmful water pollutants
    D. elimination of water pollutants categorized as *most dangerous* by the Environmental Protection Agency

    21.____

22. The process by which contaminant chemicals are removed during the water treatment process is called

    A. screening   B. sedimentation
    C. straining   D. treatment

    22.____

23. All of the following are aspects of major concern in the protection of coastal basins EXCEPT

    A. changes in circulation caused by alteration of basin configuration
    B. degradation of ecological condition of basin and its margins
    C. loss of ecologically vital areas
    D. salinity of basin waters

    23.____

24. The process of lime coagulation is used to remove _____ from a water supply.   24._____
   A. phosphates   B. lead
   C. nitrates   D. iron

25. Of the following, the LEAST effective method for controlling the effect of automotive emissions has been   25._____
   A. parking restrictions in urban areas
   B. carpooling incentives
   C. modification of liquid fuels
   D. toll bridges and highways

KEY (CORRECT ANSWERS)

1. B	11. A
2. B	12. C
3. B	13. B
4. C	14. A
5. D	15. A
6. B	16. C
7. D	17. D
8. B	18. D
9. A	19. A
10. B	20. C

21. B
22. D
23. D
24. A
25. C

EXAMINATION SECTION
TEST 1

DIRECTIONS: Each question or incomplete statement is followed by several suggested answers or completions. Select the one that BEST answers the question or completes the statement. *PRINT THE LETTER OF THE CORRECT ANSWER IN THE SPACE AT THE RIGHT.*

1. Which of the following devices has the HIGHEST energy efficiency?   1.____

    A. Diesel engine
    B. Small electric motor
    C. Home gas furnace
    D. Solar cell

2. A change in the quality of an environment, caused by an increase in temperature, is called   2.____

    A. thermal pollution
    B. oxidation
    C. thermodynamics
    D. transpiration

3. Which of the following industries places the HIGHEST energy demands on the environment?   3.____

    A. Food production and processing
    B. Paper and related products
    C. Stone, clay, glass, and concrete production
    D. Chemicals and chemical products

4. The environmental influence responsible for more human illness than any other factor is   4.____

    A. nuclear waste
    B. air pollution
    C. acid rain
    D. water pollution

5. Which of the following is NOT a difficulty involved in putting wind energy to use?   5.____

    A. Harnessing the three-dimensional dispersion of wind
    B. Finding locations that are consistently windy enough to be useful
    C. Erratic and variable speeds of most winds
    D. Inefficient transmission of energy from collection sites to populations

6. Which of the following classes of insecticides will break down MOST quickly after their use?   6.____

    A. Chlorinated hydrocarbons, such as DDT
    B. Botanicals, such as Rotenone
    C. Organophosphates, such as Malathion
    D. Carbamates, such as Sevin

7. In harvesting coal from the earth, the difference between tunnel and strip mining is that strip mining   7.____

    A. is more expensive
    B. is less efficient
    C. is more likely to cause soil erosion
    D. disrupts the flow of ground water

8. The MAIN portion of metallic lead toxins are produced by

   A. paint products
   B. automobile emissions
   C. commercial pesticides
   D. home electricity

9. What is the common name for a heat pump that heats the exterior at the expense of the interior?

   A. Furnace
   B. Generator
   C. Refrigerator
   D. Turbine

10. Artificially raising the temperature of aquatic environments has a negative effect on aquatic organisms because

    A. some organisms become infertile at warmer temperatures
    B. warm water carries less oxygen than cold
    C. the mobility of larger organisms is decreased
    D. warm water interferes with the photosynthesis of microorganisms

11. The type of energy source that does NOT add additional heat to the environment is

    A. solar
    B. fossil fuel
    C. hydroelectric
    D. tidal

12. Which of the following is NOT a drawback involved with the use of agricultural insecticides?

    A. Gradual acquisition of immunity by pest populations
    B. The loss of beneficial insects, such as wasps
    C. Eventual damage to plant matter in crops
    D. Environmental contamination from chemical residues

13. Radiation that arises from natural radioactive materials that are ALWAYS present in the environment is called

    A. background radiation
    B. ionizing radiation
    C. backfill
    D. alpha radiation

14. The INITIAL factor in the formation of natural oil and gas deposits is

    A. large accumulations of organic matter
    B. seismic activity beneath the earth"s surface
    C. drying-out of large bodies of water
    D. volcanic mixture of earthly minerals

15. What is the APPROXIMATE percentage of air pollutants, by weight, that come directly from automobiles?

    A. 10%   B. 40%   C. 65%   D. 80%

16. In detergents, the additives that extract minerals from washing water are

    A. enzymes
    B. lyes
    C. phosphates
    D. nitrates

17. Which of the following methods of transportation requires the LOWEST expense of energy per person/passenger? 17.____

    A. Walking
    B. Train
    C. Intercity bus
    D. Bicycle

18. Which of the following chemical compounds is a component of acid rain? 18.____

    A. Hydrogen sulfide
    B. Carbon monoxide
    C. Hydrocarbon
    D. Sulfur dioxide

19. Most of the electricity used in the United States today is generated by 19.____

    A. solar cells
    B. tidal generators
    C. steam turbines
    D. internal combustion engines

20. Which of the following methods of municipal waste is MOST harmful to the environment and surrounding populations? 20.____

    A. Open dumping
    B. Sanitary landfill
    C. Incineration
    D. Incineration and ocean dumping

21. Which of the following is NOT a problem posed by the construction of hydroelectric dams? 21.____

    A. Wildlife habitat destruction
    B. Water loss through evaporation
    C. Total obstruction of seasonal water flow
    D. Silting-up of reservoirs

22. Each of the following is a principal constituent of fertilizer runoff EXCEPT 22.____

    A. hydrocarbons
    B. nitrates
    C. potash
    D. phosphates

23. Of the following, which industry is responsible for the GREATEST amount of hazardous wastes imposed upon the environment? 23.____

    A. Organic chemicals, pesticides, and explosives
    B. Pharmaceuticals
    C. Petroleum refining
    D. Smelting and refining of primary metals

24. Which of the following is a non-renewable energy resource? 24.____

    A. Tidal currents
    B. Natural oil/gas deposits
    C. Solar heat
    D. Geothermal energy

25. The suspension of air pollutants in the atmosphere near the earth's surface is caused by 25.____

    A. littoral drift
    B. convection
    C. thermal inversion
    D. acid rain

KEY (CORRECT ANSWERS)

1. C
2. A
3. D
4. D
5. B

6. B
7. C
8. B
9. C
10. B

11. A
12. C
13. A
14. A
15. B

16. C
17. D
18. D
19. C
20. A

21. C
22. A
23. A
24. B
25. C

TEST 2

DIRECTIONS: Each question or incomplete statement is followed by several suggested answers or completions. Select the one that BEST answers the question or completes the statement. *PRINT THE LETTER OF THE CORRECT ANSWER IN THE SPACE AT THE RIGHT.*

1. Which of the following sources is responsible for the GREATEST level of ozone depletion in the earth's atmosphere?

    A. Aerosol propellants
    B. Commercial and residential refrigeration
    C. Production of plastic foam and insulation
    D. Solvent cleaning of metal and electronic parts

    1.____

2. High concentrations of mercury and aluminum in soil are caused by

    A. acid contamination
    B. plant respiration
    C. ammonia seepage
    D. natural decomposition

    2.____

3. Which of the following waste products is MOST abundant in landfill sites?

    A. Paper products
    B. Plastics
    C. Glass
    D. Metals

    3.____

4. Which of the following types of cells are LEAST susceptible to contamination from nuclear waste?

    A. Reproductive
    B. Blood
    C. Lymph
    D. Nerve

    4.____

5. Which of the following effects is caused by the runoff of agricultural fertilizers into surface water supplies?

    A. Sterilization of larger aquatic vertebrates
    B. Killing algae and other microorganisms
    C. Increasing mercury content
    D. Eventual depletion of oxygen

    5.____

6. Traditionally, most low-level nuclear wastes produced in the United States have been disposed of

    A. in deep formations of stable rock
    B. under sheets of polar ice
    C. in shallow land-burial sites
    D. far into the open sea

    6.____

7. Which of the following is the result of atmospheric decomposition that comes from emissions of sulfur dioxide and oxides of nitrogen?

    A. Ozone depletion
    B. Smog
    C. Fermentation
    D. Acid rain

    7.____

8. Highly toxic chemicals, such as PCBs, that are the byproducts of manufacturing processes or waste-burning are called

   A. hydrocarbons
   B. solvents
   C. dioxins
   D. fluorocarbons

9. Which of the following is NOT a potential source of fossil fuel?

   A. Iron ore
   B. Tar sand
   C. Shale
   D. Underground methane

10. Each of the following is considered an effective material for lining the disposal sites of toxic wastes EXCEPT

    A. clay
    B. rubber
    C. plastic
    D. sandstone

11. Which energy source presents the GREATEST risk to workers involved in the entire process of energy production?

    A. Coal
    B. Oil
    C. Natural gas
    D. Uranium

12. Water vapor that has collected around microscopic particles of air pollution is described as

    A. smog
    B. acid rain
    C. haze
    D. particulate

13. The PRIMARY stage of municipal sewage treatment removes which of the following elements from sewage?

    A. Dissolved chemicals
    B. Grit and coarse solids
    C. Sediments
    D. Microorganisms

14. Introducing microbes that feed on water contaminants into a polluted body of water is an example of

    A. adsorption
    B. bioremediation
    C. desalinization
    D. integrated pest control

15. Producing energy by splitting the nucleus of a single radioactive atom is called

    A. radiation
    B. nuclear fission
    C. neutron chain reaction
    D. nuclear fusion

16. Which of the following is NOT a source of acid precipitation?

    A. Automobile emissions
    B. Nuclear power generation
    C. Coal-burning stoves
    D. Electrical plants powered by steam turbines

17. Currently, the LEAST plentiful energy source available to the United States from our natural reserves is

    A. petroleum
    B. natural gas
    C. coal
    D. uranium oxide

18. Which of the following chemical compounds is a PRIMARY cause of ozone depletion? 18.____

    A. Nitrogen oxide
    B. Bicarbonate
    C. Dioxin
    D. Chlorofluorocarbon

19. Which of the following is a function performed by a solar collector? 19.____

    A. Heating water
    B. Using sunlight to ignite combustible materials
    C. Converting sunlight to electricity
    D. Storing energy

20. Sulfur dioxide, a poisonous gas, is produced by the 20.____

    A. use of aerosol sprays
    B. evaporation of acid-contaminated waters
    C. burning of coal
    D. upwelling of poorly-contained nuclear wastes

21. Which of the following is an example of *point source* water pollution? 21.____

    A. Agricultural runoff into streams
    B. Seepage of industrial chemicals into groundwater supplies
    C. An oil spill caused by the wreck of a tanker
    D. Acid rain contamination of a large lake

22. Which non-chemical pollutant has proven MOST hazardous to marine and aquatic wildlife? 22.____

    A. Metals
    B. Paper products
    C. Plastics
    D. Construction by-products

23. Most of the thermoplastics produced in the United States are from which of the following categories? 23.____

    A. Polyethylene
    B. Polystyrene
    C. Polypropylene
    D. Polyurethane

24. Each of the following is an example of a *soft* energy resource EXCEPT 24.____

    A. geothermal heat
    B. wind energy
    C. natural gas deposits
    D. solar power

25. Which type of coal has the GREATEST heating potential? 25.____

    A. Bituminous
    B. Anthracite
    C. Subbituminous
    D. Lignite

KEY (CORRECT ANSWERS)

1. C
2. A
3. A
4. D
5. D

6. C
7. D
8. C
9. A
10. D

11. A
12. C
13. B
14. B
15. B

16. B
17. A
18. D
19. A
20. C

21. C
22. C
23. A
24. C
25. B

EXAMINATION SECTION
TEST 1

DIRECTIONS: Each question or incomplete statement is followed by several suggested answers or completions. Select the one that BEST answers the question or completes the statement. *PRINT THE LETTER OF THE CORRECT ANSWER IN THE SPACE AT THE RIGHT.*

1. Which of the following devices is considered to be the MOST effective way of reporting a water supply's chemical composition data?

    A. table
    B. bar graph
    C. cross-referenced spread sheet
    D. circular graph

    1.____

2. The type of data report which MUST be used as an integral part of any dataprocessing system associated with air quality measurement is

    A. data summarization
    B. diurnal variation pattern
    C. pollutant rose
    D. frequency distribution

    2.____

3. The term for an analyst's attempt to detect and correct any errors that have entered the data set is data

    A. handling
    B. validation
    C. processing
    D. proofing

    3.____

4. Of the types of data listed below, which one is NOT used as a parameter to define the physical characteristics of a lake?

    A. Surface area
    B. Average depth
    C. Underlying rock characteristics
    D. Retention time

    4.____

5. The difference between the least and greatest values in a data set is known as the set's

    A. variance   B. range   C. mean deviation   D. mode

    5.____

6. When experts in the same field disagree about conclusions drawn from a set of environmental impact assessment data, they sometimes privately answer a prepared questionnaire, and then distribute a summary sheet of opposing viewpoints amongst themselves. This method is known as

    A. the cooperative assessment model
    B. the Delphi technique
    C. the operational gaming model
    D. collective data validation

    6.____

7. The term for calculated decrease In water pressure within a delivery system is

    A. vacuum   B. head loss   C. backup   D. flow gradient

    7.____

8. Of the types of environmental impact data variables below, the one which is an example of an output variable is

    A. effects on natural and social environments
    B. population projections
    C. transportation networks
    D. economic growth

    8.____

27

9. All of the following are factors required for the calculation of flow velocity in water delivery systems EXCEPT

   A. quantity of flow
   B. pipe material
   C. slope of hydraulic gradient
   D. temperature of flow

10. _____ errors in a data set are MOST easily estimated by the use of standard statistical techniques.

    A. Systematic   B. Random   C. Clerical   D. Standard

11. The one of the following which Is NOT an element of the data base needed in order to make decisions about water quality control is the

    A. physical characteristics of the water resource
    B. local needs and desires concerning use
    C. projected quality of untreated water
    D. present uses of resource

12. The air quality data report that consists of collected averages for a specific daily time period is the

    A. pollutant rose
    B. data summarization
    C. diurnal variation pattern
    D. frequency distribution

13. The concentration of bacteriological wastes in water is USUALLY expressed in terms of

    A. parts per million
    B. specific particle ratios, depending on the waste
    C. kiloPascals
    D. BOD

14. The one of the characteristics below that Is NOT used as a criterion for determining the quality of a data set is

    A. flexibility
    B. representativeness
    C. comparability
    D. completeness

15. In water delivery systems, water pressure is USUALLY measured in units called

    A. meters of head
    B. pounds per square inch
    C. flow gradients
    D. Pascals

16. In measuring air quality, extremes in data are often due to each of the following EXCEPT

    A. meteorological factors
    B. clerical misrecordings
    C. lab errors
    D. saturation of continuous data

17. The term for the difference between a data set's MEASURED and REFERENCED values is

    A. accuracy
    B. quantitative error
    C. reliability
    D. precision

18. In order to determine the storage needed to equalize a community's water supply demand at a constant pumping pressure, the MOST important data set needed is the

    A. exact pumping pressure
    B. time of daily peak use
    C. community's consumption rate
    D. delivery time between source and key use stations

19. _____ is the MOST commonly used method for determining the central value of a given data set.

    A. Mid-range
    B. Mode
    C. Arithmetic mean
    D. Median

20. What is the method for determining the standard deviation of values in a data set?

    A. Square root of the variance
    B. Half the total variance
    C. Average of all deviating values
    D. Average of the square roots of all deviating values

21. The MOST commonly used device for recording and reporting water delivery data at household sites is the

    A. compound meter
    B. digital register
    C. current meter
    D. disk meter

22. The term for the air quality data report that summarizes how often concentrations of specific magnitudes occur is

    A. frequency distribution
    B. data summarization
    C. pollutant rose
    D. diurnal variation pattern

23. Regarding environmental impact assessment, the goal of relating input and output variables in a data set is to

    A. validate the data set
    B. understand the consequences of imposing alternative policies
    C. establish a consensus about policy objectives
    D. compile an adequately useful data set

24. In order to calculate the intake capacity for a fire flow water delivery system, an analyst should compare the system's

    A. average pressure to the average distance of delivery
    B. total storage to the maximum amount of water needed
    C. maximum pressure to the maximum distance of delivery
    D. total storage to the average amount of water needed

25. Which of the distorting factors below is almost EXCLUSIVELY involved with the presentation of data, rather than the documentation?

    A. Mechanical error
    B. Bias
    C. Meteorological factors
    D. Clerical error

KEY (CORRECT ANSWERS)

1.	B	11.	C
2.	A	12.	C
3.	B	13.	D
4.	C	14.	A
5.	B	15.	A
6.	B	16.	D
7.	B	17.	A
8.	A	18.	C
9.	D	19.	C
10.	B	20.	A

21. D
22. A
23. B
24. B
25. B

TEST 2

DIRECTIONS: Each, question or incomplete statement is followed by several suggested answers or completions. Select the one that BEST answers the question or completes the statement. *PRINT THE LETTER OF THE CORRECT ANSWER IN THE SPACE AT THE RIGHT.*

1. The determination of a drinking water supply's conformity with established bacteriological requirements is based on

    A. comparisons with dissolved solids data
    B. correlated oxygen content
    C. average measurement readings of all tests performed
    D. the number of positive tests

    1.____

2. The magnitude of error associated with a particular data set is known as

    A. systematic error
    B. data quality
    C. standard variance
    D. standard error

    2.____

3. Which type of air quality data report uses a circular figure for presentation, rather than a table or graph?

    A. Diurnal variation pattern
    B. Pollutant rose
    C. Frequency distribution
    D. Data summarization

    3.____

4. When the water pressure within a delivery system is greater than the atmospheric pressure, it is called

    A. gage pressure
    B. barometric pressure
    C. vacuum
    D. absolute pressure

    4.____

5. In data evaluation, the term for the variability of measurements of the same quantity gathered using the same method is

    A. standard deviation
    B. precision
    C. accuracy
    D. data variability

    5.____

6. The data used as the PRIMARY criterion for determining the amount of an allowable Industrial waste dump into a flowing stream is

    A. external climatic factors
    B. projected flow of the watercourse
    C. biotic potential of surrounding waters
    D. toxicity of waste material

    6.____

7. Once the data have been gathered for an environmental impact assessment, experts play a prominent role in each of the following ways, EXCEPT

    A. identifying alternatives and control variables
    B. relating input to output variables
    C. gathering more data using techniques of greater refinement
    D. evaluating reliability and applicability of data

    7.____

8. In determining the quality of a given water sample, concentrations of dissolved elements are expressed in terms of:

   A. volume
   B. mass
   C. particle ratios
   D. surface area

9. The errors in a data set that CANNOT be estimated by the use of standard statistical techniques, and usually produce a biased result, are called _____ errors.

   A. systematic
   B. random
   C. clerical
   D. standard

10. The method for data presentation MOST commonly used to illustrate the relationship between two sets of continuous data is the

    A. bar chart
    B. histogram
    C. block graph
    D. scatter diagram

11. _____ consumption is NOT part of the data set needed to quantitatively evaluate a community's water use.

    A. Average daily
    B. Peak hourly
    C. Peak daily
    D. Average hourly

12. The precision of a data set is BEST expressed in terms of

    A. mode
    B. standard deviation
    C. average
    D. frequency

13. In water delivery systems, the use of a manometer for measuring water pressure is

    A. usually limited to indoor, fixed units
    B. a universally adopted practice
    C. most commonly applied to mobile units
    D. seldom used indoors

14. All of the following are problems often associated with the practice of intermittently collecting air quality data EXCEPT

    A. inaccurate averages
    B. increased likelihood of extreme values
    C. greater meteorological impact on data
    D. increased susceptibility to error

15. Which of the following Is NOT a method used to measure variation within a data set?

    A. Mean deviation
    B. Standard deviation
    C. Range
    D. Variance mode

16. The device MOST commonly used to report pipe flow data for a water delivery system is the

    A. table
    B. circular graph
    C. cross-referenced spread sheet
    D. nomograph

17. Of the following, the one which is NOT a problem often associated with using the operational gaming model for evaluating environmental impact assessment data is

    A. distancing of interested parties
    B. increased adventurousness of field experts
    C. introduction of human behavioral patterns into the assessment
    D. possibly inaccurate idealization of the system

18. The chemical analysis of a water sample can be used to determine each of the following factors EXCEPT

    A. dissolved solids
    B. alkalinity
    C. biotic potential
    D. pH

19. The air quality data report that groups data according to prevailing wind directions is the

    A. frequency distribution
    B. pollutant rose
    C. diurnal variation pattern
    D. data summarization

20. The MOST commonly used device for measuring water pressure in delivery systems is the

    A. piezometer
    B. Bourdon gauge
    C. manometer
    D. barometric gauge

21. Each of the following is a problem associated with the use of existing data in making environmental impact assessments EXCEPT the

    A. possibility of different gathering techniques
    B. uncertainty of data accuracy due to time lapse
    C. unsuitability of data for an analyst's specific purpose
    D. personal bias of the analyst using the data

22. The data presentation method that works BEST for illustrating frequency distributions is the

    A. compass graph
    B. table
    C. histogram
    D. bar graph

23. The _____ is NOT a factor required in order to calculate storm runoff.

    A. maximum flow rate
    B. area's average rainfall intensity
    C. type and character of runoff surface
    D. minimum flow rate

24. Which of the characteristics of a data set is almost EXCLUSIVELY involved in the documentation of values, rather than the presentation?

    A. Accuracy
    B. Representativeness
    C. Bias
    D. Comparability

25. The MOST frequently appearing value in a data set is known as its

    A. variance standard
    B. mode
    C. mid-range
    D. median

KEY (CORRECT ANSWERS)

1. D
2. B
3. B
4. A
5. B

6. B
7. C
8. B
9. A
10. D

11. D
12. B
13. A
14. C
15. D

16. D
17. A
18. C
19. B
20. B

21. D
22. C
23. D
24. A
25. B

EXAMINATION SECTION
TEST 1

DIRECTIONS: Each question or incomplete statement is followed by several suggested answers or completions. Select the one that BEST answers the question or completes the statement. *PRINT THE LETTER OF THE CORRECT ANSWER IN THE SPACE AT THE RIGHT.*

1. Ebenezer Howard is BEST known for the concept of self-sufficient towns with mixed economies which are called

   A. new towns
   B. garden cities
   C. planned unit developments
   D. suburbs

2. The new town of Columbia, Maryland, has which of the following planned features?
   I. Neighborhood clusters
   II. A rail commuter system
   III. Prior land assembly
   IV. Prohibition of industry
   The CORRECT answer is:

   A. II only   B. I, III   C. II, IV   D. I, III, IV

3. The two lines on the graph shown at the right BEST represent which of the following combinations of travel behavior in a metropolitan area of 2 million population?

   A. Transit and private automobile trips
   B. Weekday and weekend trips
   C. All work and nonwork trips
   D. Office and retail-generated trips

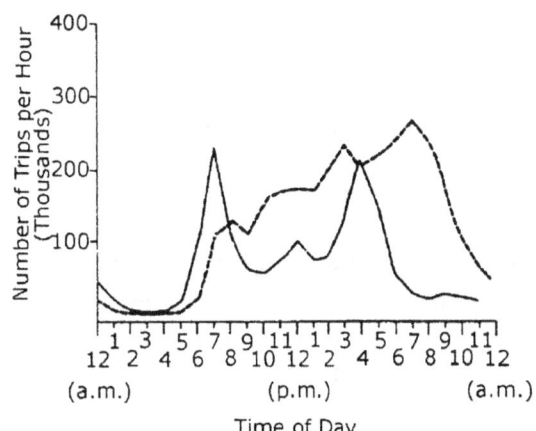

4. Assume that you are the director of a local planning agency, and that you recognize the interdependency of the chief executive, the planning agency, operating departments, and independent boards and commissions. In a hypothetical situation, a proposed expansion of a county airport and adjacent industrial areas is in opposition to the planning agency's proposal for a regional park location.
The planning agency believes there are unique circumstances and sound reasons for preferring the regional park proposal along with future relocation of the airport to another site in the county.
Which of the following strategies would likely place you, as the planning director, in the LEAST effective coordinating role in resolving the conflict?

A. Attempting to have the planning agency solely responsible for additional studies and recommendations
B. Directing planning staff to discontinue all studies of this issue and direct all inquiries regarding this matter to the director
C. Recommending the study control be given to the staff of the chief executive's office
D. Soliciting support of other departments and agencies for the planning agency's regional park proposal

5. Recent major developments in household characteristics in the United States have been characterized by which of the following?
   I. A marked increase in nonfamily living arrangements among the adult population has been observed in recent years.
   II. A major development in marriage trends has been the sharply decreasing level of divorce in central cities.
   III. Families (households where all members are related) maintained by either men or women who have no spouse living with them represent a growing proportion of all family households.
   IV. After several decades of decline in household size, the number of persons per unit has increased in metropolitan area since 1970.

   The CORRECT answer is:

   A. I only   B. I, III   C. III, IV   D. I, II, IV

5.____

Questions 6-9.

DIRECTIONS: The group of questions below consists of four lettered headings followed by a list of numbered phrases. For each numbered phrase, select the one heading which is MOST closely related to it. One heading may be used once, more than once, or not at all.

In the following list, which of the formal bodies that operate within a city most likely would take final action on each of the following requests?

   A. City Council
   B. City Court
   C. Board of Zoning Appeals
   D. School Board

6. A request to acquire land for a new school.   6.____

7. A request to condemn property in a blighted area.   7.____

8. A request to levy a special property assessment for a street.   8.____

9. A request for a variance from a zoning ordinance.   9.____

10. In reference to the following hypothetical linear regression equation that describes household trip generation with the census tract as the unit of analysis, which of the following statements about R^2 is CORRECT?

   $T = -.65 + .96(p) + .61(v)$
   $R^2 = .69$
   T = the average number of daily vehicle trips from home per DU (dwelling unit)
   p = persons per DU
   v = vehicles per DU

   A. It shows that more p causes households to make more trips.
   B. It shows that more p, only when coupled with more automobiles, causes households to make more trips.
   C. It indicates that 69% of the variation in trip generation is explained by p and v.
   D. There is a 45% probability that the variables T, p, and v are correlated by chance.

10.____

Questions 11-14.

DIRECTIONS: Questions 11 through 14 are to be answered on the basis of the following circumstance.

The desirability and feasibility of a proposed shopping center are to be evaluated. The primary concerns are that conditions of the city zoning ordinance be met and that the project be a profitable venture. The developer owns a 30-acre parcel and proposes to construct a 250,000-square foot leasable area with 1,300 on-site parking spaces. The shopping center will serve a trade area that contains 20,000 households. The average household disposable income is $12,000. The shopping center will have a 50:50 split of square footage between convenience and shopper's goods.

11. Which of the following would be APPROPRIATE in a shopping center of this size?

    A. A major grocery and a drugstore as prime tenants
    B. Either a department or discount store as the anchor tenant
    C. Three department stores of approximately the same size
    D. A series of smaller stores rather than an anchor tenant

11.____

12. If an average of 400 square feet is needed to accommodate each parking space and associated driveways, the APPROXIMATE acreage of the blacktop area of the site would be _____ acres.

    A. Less than 10   B. Between 10 and 15
    C. Between 15 and 20   D. More than 20

12.____

13. If 50 percent of disposable income is allocated to retail purchases, a minimum of $100 of sales per square foot is needed to operate profitably, and 750,000 square feet of retail business already exists in the trade area, which of the following should be concluded? The

    A. trade area is already overbuilt and cannot support additional development without further population growth
    B. new shopping center will use up all of the untapped purchasing power of the trade area

13.____

C. existing and proposed centers can operate profitably with excess purchasing power available for additional development
D. trade area is not overbuilt presently, but it can only accommodate an additional 150,000 square feet

14. Provisions in the zoning ordinance require a 4:1 ratioof open space to building space and a 5:1,000-square foot ratio of parking space to gross leasable area (GLA). According to the ordinance, which of the following statements about the parcel is CORRECT?
It is

   A. too small to accommodate the projected center, although adequate parking would be provided
   B. large enough to accommodate the projected center, but parking spaces would be inadequate
   C. large enough to accommodate the projected center, and sufficient parking would be provided
   D. grossly underutilized and could accommodate additional square footage and additional parking spaces

14.____

Questions 15-17.

DIRECTIONS: Questions 15 through 17 are to be answered on the basis of the following information.

Planners in a large city that consists of 150 neighborhoods are concerned about the provision and allocation of health-care clinics at the multiple-neighborhood level throughout the city. One of the main concerns is prenatal health care. Variables relevant to this situation are as follows:

QPNHC = the overall quality of prenatal health care
IMR = the percentage of children who survive their first three months of life (a type of infant mortality rate) and who were born in the same one-year period
NWP = the number of women pregnant at any time during a one-year period
NA = the number of appointments kept at the health clinic per year
FI = the family incomes of residents in thousands of dollars ($1,000's)
D = the distance of families from the health clinics in miles

(Neighborhood averages can be generated for each of these variables.)

15. The planners have decided that the neighborhood infant mortality rate will serve as the operational objective of the prenatal health care system.
Which of the following would be the MOST serious criticism leveled against their decision?

   A. It is impossible to calculate the IMR at the neighborhood level.
   B. The data on the use of the clinic (NA) are easier to obtain and more accurate than the other data.
   C. The IMR is a good quantitative but weak qualitative index of the QPNHC.
   D. The collection of IMR data is irrelevant to the problem.

15.____

16. Which of the following is an output variable within the model?

   A. IMR   B. NWP   C. FI   D. D

16.____

17. It is now 10 years later; the clinics were built and a very comprehensive data collection system was kept in operation. The clinic programs are under fire, the budgets are expected to be slashed, and some clinics probably will be forced to close. Time is short. Based on this situation, which of the following would be the LEAST critical evaluation question?

    A. Are higher levels of clinic usage associated with various infant mortality rates?
    B. If distance does not affect the use of the clinics, does it do so differentially by income strata?
    C. What kinds of persons (education, income level, etc.) use each clinic?
    D. Are family income levels associated with distance

KEY (CORRECT ANSWERS)

1. B
2. B
3. C
4. B
5. B

6. D
7. A
8. A
9. C
10. C

11. B
12. B
13. C
14. C
15. C
16. A
17. D

EXAMINATION SECTION
TEST 1

DIRECTIONS: Each question or incomplete statement is followed by several suggested answers or completions. Select the one that BEST answers the question or completes the statement. *PRINT THE LETTER OF THE CORRECT ANSWER IN THE SPACE AT THE RIGHT.*

1. A single sample acceptance sampling plan and a double sampling plan, used by a city agency to accept paving materials, have identical O.C. curves.
   This implies that

   A. the double sampling plan offers vendors greater protection
   B. the double sampling plan offers the city greater protection
   C. both sampling plans offer vendors equal protection
   D. the double sampling plan has greater power

1.____

2. Which one of the following factors would be of NO importance in a time-series analysis of monthly sales, in kilowatt hours of electricity billed, of Consolidated Edison Company from 2015 to 2016?

   A. Price level variation
   B. Secular trend
   C. Cyclical variation
   D. Seasonal variation

2.____

3. A scatter diagram indicates that a straight line would offer a good description of the relationship between two variables.
   In this case, the number of lines about which the sum of the deviations is zero is

   A. 0
   B. 1
   C. infinite
   D. equal to the number of pairs of observations

3.____

Questions 4-7.

DIRECTIONS: Questions 4 through 7 are to be answered on the basis of the following information.

A sample survey was conducted in Williamsburg to determine the attitude of residents toward the erection of a state office building in the area. The number of responses by character of response and by age group follows.

Response	Age 18 and under 25	Age 25 and under 50	Age 50 or over	Total
Opposed	50	10	10	70
Neutral	25	30	15	70
Favorable	5	40	15	60
Total	80	80	40	200

4. To test whether there is a significant difference between the total number favorable and the total number opposed, you should use the _____ distribution.

   A. t
   B. Poisson
   C. exponential
   D. binomial

5. In testing for independence between response and age with the use of the Chi-square distribution, the CORRECT number of degrees of freedom is

   A. 1 B. 4 C. 6 D. D, 9

6. In testing the hypothesis of independence, the expected number of favorable responses among the 50-or-over age group is

   A. 10 B. 12 C. 15 D. 24

7. If the Chi-square test results in the rejection of the test for independence, we may conclude that response and age _____ variables.

   A. are not correlated
   B. are correlated
   C. may or may not be correlated
   D. are both continuous

Questions 8-10.

DIRECTIONS: Questions 8 through 10 are to be answered on the basis of the following passage.

Assume that you have given a typing test to a random sample of 30 typists before and after taking a special course in typing. The results of this experiment are to be used to determine whether to undertake a large scale training program for typists by the city.

8. The experiment offers an illustration of

   A. non-linear estimation
   B. matched pairs
   C. Poisson process
   D. unmatched pairs

9. In testing whether typing skills improve on the average after training, the PROPER number of degrees of freedom for a t test is

   A. 29 B. 30 C. 59 D. 60

10. The estimate of the standard error of the difference between the sample means, before and after training, does NOT depend upon the _____ training.

    A. variance of the population test scores before
    B. variance of the population test scores after
    C. correlation between the populations' test scores before and after
    D. mean of the population before

11. The probability of receiving a parking ticket for illegal parking has been estimated at .50. How many times must a car be illegally parked before that probability of being ticketed at least once exceeds .90, assuming that successive trials are independent?

A. Once B. Twice
C. Three times D. Four times

12. If an artificial variable appears in the solution to a linear programming problem as a positive basic variable, it indicates

    A. a poor choice of the artificial variable
    B. the need for a non-linear programming solution
    C. the absence of a feasible solution
    D. that there must have been an error in computation

13. Exponential smoothing as a forecasting technique is often used because it

    A. automatically adjusts for trend
    B. can be used only with annual data
    C. involves equal weights to all preceding years
    D. involves greater weighting of more recent years

14. The coefficient of variation of times parked by cars at parking meters, measured in minutes, is 36 percent.
    If the times parked were measured in hours, the coefficient of variation would be _____ percent.

    A. 0.6   B. 3.6   C. 6   D. 36

15. Six *t*-tests, each at the .10 level of significance, are used to test the significance of the 6 possible differences among 4 sample means.
    The probability of rejecting the null hypothesis of no difference among the pairs of sample means at least once is APPROXIMATELY

    A. .47   B. .53   C. .81   D. .90

16. A study is made to determine whether the rate of unemployment has changed significantly during the past year. A characteristic of studies of this type is that they involve a(n)

    A. one-tailed test
    B. two-tailed test
    C. alpha-risk greater than the beta-risk
    D. beta-risk greater than the alpha-risk

17. In determining the size of the sample needed to achieve a 5 percent error in the estimate of the length of a cab ride in a central business district on the basis of a simple random sample of cab rides, a population standard deviation of 0.5 miles is assumed. On the basis of this study, the estimate of the standard deviation of the population is 0.375 miles. On the basis of this information, it is generally TRUE that

    A. the sample was improperly drawn
    B. greater precision was obtained than planned
    C. you should have used a larger sample
    D. a .95 confidence interval will have too great a range

18. The three costs usually associated with an inventory model are: (1) shortage costs, (2) replenishment costs, and the third is _____ costs.

    A. fixed   B. variable   C. holding   D. expected

Questions 19-20.

DIRECTIONS: Questions 19 and 20 are to be answered on the basis of the following information.

A municipal swimming pool has the following revenue (R) and cost (C) functions:
R = 900X
C = 100 + 800X, where X is the proportion of utilization of the facility

19. What value of X maximizes R-C?

    A. 0
    B. 1/2
    C. 3/4
    D. 1

20. The value of R-C is

    A. never positive
    B. never negative
    C. 900X
    D. always positive

KEY (CORRECT ANSWERS)

1.	C	11.	D
2.	A	12.	C
3.	C	13.	D
4.	D	14.	D
5.	B	15.	A
6.	B	16.	B
7.	B	17.	B
8.	B	18.	C
9.	A	19.	D
10.	D	20.	A

TEST 2

DIRECTIONS: Each question or incomplete statement is followed by several suggested answers or completions. Select the one that BEST answers the question or completes the statement. *PRINT THE LETTER OF THE CORRECT ANSWER IN THE SPACE AT THE RIGHT.*

1. The one of the following statements concerning linear programming problems which is NOT correct is that such problems 1.____

    A. always have duals
    B. always have finite solutions
    C. sometimes have more than one solution
    D. have linear objective functions

2. Which of the following is NOT an optimization technique? _____ programming. 2.____

    A. Integer   B. Geometric   C. Linear   D. Computer

Question 3.

DIRECTIONS: Consider the inventory model where the optimal order quantity is given by $\sqrt{\frac{2Ds}{PI}}$ and where D = the demand rate, s = the set-up cost per cycle, p = the price of the item, and I = the carrying cost rate.

3. What change in the price of the item causes the optimal order quantity to double? 3.____

    A. Doubling of the price   B. A 50% reduction
    C. A 75% reduction   D. Cannot be determined

4. In considering the following populations corresponding to employees of a given agency: job title, sex, age, income, and height, which one of the following contains ONLY qualitative populations? 4.____

    A. Age, income, height   B. Job title and sex
    C. Sex and age   D. Job title and income

5. The relative frequency of Puerto Rican children in an elementary school of 1600 pupils is .015. 5.____
   The number of Puerto Rican pupils in the school is

    A. 240   B. 200   C. 150   D. 24

Questions 6-8.

DIRECTIONS: Questions 6 through 8 are to be answered on the basis of the following network. Activity time is indicated in days.

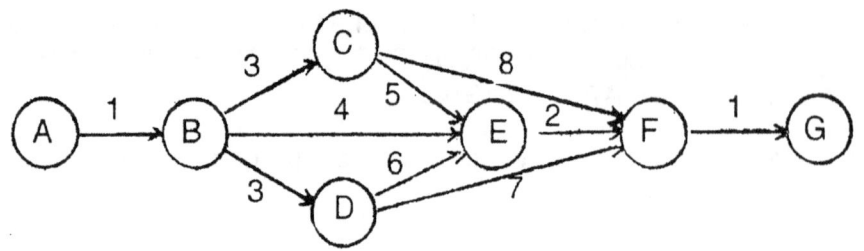

6. The number of paths through the network is 6._____

   A. 6 B. 5 C. 4 D. 3

7. Which one of the following sequences of events is on the critical path? 7._____

   A. ABEFG B. ABDEFG C. ABDFG D. ABCEFG

8. The EARLIEST completion for the project, in days, is 8._____

   A. 8 B. 13 C. 15 D. 17

9. A quarterly seasonal index of absenteeism among employees in the department of sanitation has been computed. Which of the following seasonal index series is the CORRECT one? 9._____

	SEASONAL INDEX		
1stQ	2ndQ	3rdQ	4thQ
A. 104	106	98	96
B. 102	98	104	100
C. -10	+12	+5	-6
D. -10	-8	+6	+12

10. In inventory problems, a decrease in the fixed set-up costs GENERALLY 10._____

    A. decreases the Economic Order Quantity
    B. increases the Economic Order Quantity
    C. has no effect on the Economic Order Quantity
    D. cannot be determined in the abstract

11. If a random sample of 900 families was used to estimate the average family income and average family expenditure on food in Washington, then 11._____

    A. the standard error of both estimates would be equal
    B. the standard error of average family income would be larger
    C. the standard error of average family expenditure on food would be larger
    D. only conclusions as to the absolute magnitude of standard errors can be drawn

Questions 12-14.

DIRECTIONS: Questions 12 through 14 are to be answered on the basis of the following information.

12. C. 20

13. C. 12.15

14. D. 4.0

15. A. it represents a straight line

16. D. Hotelling's T

17. B. it produces estimates with good statistical properties

18. B. 1; 1

19. If a researcher reported that certain test results are barely significant at the .10 level, _____ level.

   A. the null hypothesis would be rejected at the .05
   B. the null hypothesis would be accepted at the .05
   C. more information is needed to determine what decision would be reached at the .05
   D. the results would not be significant at the .15

20. Which probability distribution function has an *infinite* variance?

   A. Hypergeometric
   B. *t*
   C. Cauchy
   D. Exponential

KEY (CORRECT ANSWERS)

1.	B	11.	B
2.	D	12.	C
3.	C	13.	C
4.	B	14.	D
5.	D	15.	C
6.	B	16.	D
7.	B	17.	B
8.	B	18.	B
9.	D	19.	B
10.	A	20.	C

INTERPRETING STATISTICAL DATA GRAPHS, CHARTS AND TABLES

EXAMINATION SECTION
TEST 1

DIRECTIONS: Each question or incomplete statement is followed by several suggested answers or completions. Select the one that BEST answers the question or completes the statement. *PRINT THE LETTER OF THE CORRECT ANSWER IN THE SPACE AT THE RIGHT.*

Questions 1-3.

DIRECTIONS: Questions 1 through 3 are to be answered SOLELY on the basis of the information contained in the following chart.

CHART A
MILEAGE BETWEEN NEW YORK AND POINTS IN NEARBY CONNECTICUT

	New York	Bridge-port	Dan-bury	Hart-ford	New Haven	New London	Stam-ford	Water-bury
New York	--	61	66	115	80	132	39	91
Bridgeport	61	--	27	54	19	71	22	30
Danbury	66	27	--	57	33	85	31	30
Hartford	115	54	57	--	37	44	76	27
New Haven	80	19	33	37	--	52	41	21
New London	132	71	85	44	52	--	93	62
Stamford	39	22	31	76	41	93	--	52
Waterbury	91	30	30	27	21	62	52	--

1. According to Chart A, the TOTAL mileage on a continuous trip from New York to Danbury, to Waterbury, to New London, to New York would be _____ miles. 1.____

   A. 280   B. 290   C. 316   D. 294

2. According to Chart A, the mileage between New Haven and New London is the same as the mileage between _____ and _____. 2.____

   A. Danbury; Hartford   B. Hartford; New London
   C. Stamford; New Haven   D. Waterbury; Stamford

3. According to Chart A, which of the following pairs of cities are CLOSEST to each other? 3.____

   A. Bridgeport and Hartford   B. New York and Bridgeport
   C. Hartford and Danbury   D. New Haven and New London

KEY (CORRECT ANSWERS)

1. B
2. D
3. D

TEST 2

Questions 1-4.

DIRECTIONS: Questions 1 through 4 are to be answered SOLELY on the basis of the information given in the traffic volume table below.

TRAFFIC VOLUME COUNTS				
	Main Street		Cross Street	
Time (A.M.)	Northbound	Southbound	Eastbound	Westbound
7:00 - 7:15	100	100	70	60
7:15 - 7:30	110	100	80	70
7:30 - 7:45	150	140	110	100
7:45 - 8:00	170	160	140	130
8:00 - 8:15	210	190	120	110
8:15 - 8:30	180	170	90	80
8:30 - 8:45	160	140	70	60
8:45 - 9:00	150	160	70	50
9:00 - 9:15	140	150	50	50
9:15 - 9:30	130	120	40	20
9:30 - 9:45	120	110	30	30
9:45 - 10:00	120	100	30	30

1. The hour during which traffic, moving in both directions on Main Street, reached its PEAK was

    A. 7:30 - 8:30 B. 7:45 - 8:45
    C. 8:00 - 9:00 D. 8:15 - 9:15

2. The hour during which traffic volume, moving in both directions on Cross Street, reached its PEAK was

    A. 7:30 - 8:30 B. 7:45 - 8:45
    C. 8:00 - 9:00 D. 8:15 - 9:15

3. The HIGHEST average hourly volume over the three-hour period 7:00 to 10:00 was recorded for

    A. Main Street northbound B. Main Street southbound
    C. Cross Street eastbound D. Cross Street westbound

4. The PEAK 15-minute traffic volume for all directions of travel occurred between

    A. 7:30 - 7:45 B. 7:45 - 8:00
    C. 8:00 - 8:15 D. 8:15 - 8:30

1.____

2.____

3.____

4.____

KEY (CORRECT ANSWERS)

1. B
2. A
3. A
4. C

TEST 3

Questions 1-4.

DIRECTIONS: Questions 1 through 4 are to be answered SOLELY on the basis of the sketch below.

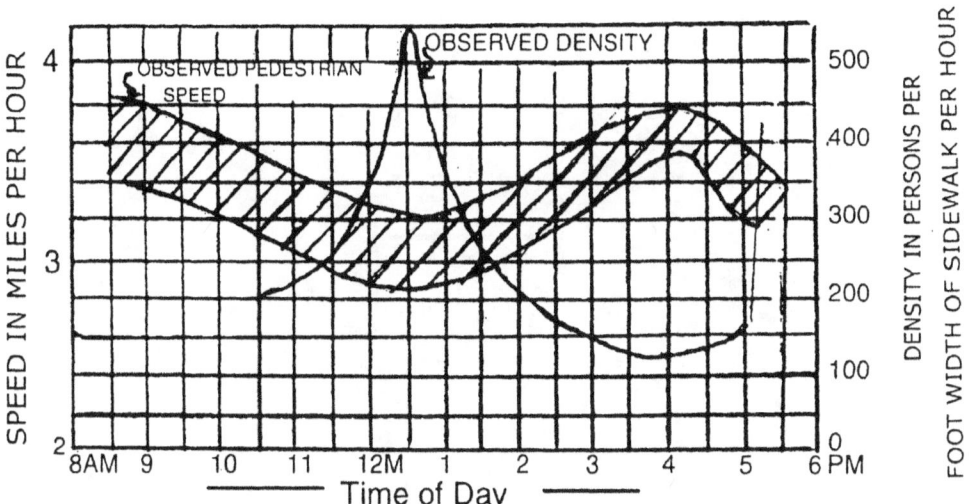

1. Assuming a 10' wide sidewalk, the number of people that would pass the given point at 12:00 Noon in 10 minutes is MOST NEARLY

   A. 580   B. 680   C. 780   D. 880

2. At 10:00 A.M., you could expect a person to be walking at a speed

   A. of 3 miles per hour
   B. between 300 and 420 feet per hour
   C. between 3.2 and 3.65 miles per hour
   D. of 4.5 feet per second

3. The highest average number of people using the sidewalk will USUALLY occur at

   A. 9 A.M.   B. 12:30 P.M.   C. 4 P.M.   D. 5 P.M.

4. Of the following statements relating to the diagram, the one that is MOST NEARLY CORRECT is

   A. the minimum walking speed observed is 2 miles per hour
   B. data for the survey was taken continuously for 24 hours
   C. as the number of people using the sidewalk increases, the speed at which they walk decreases
   D. the minimum observed density is 300 people per hour per foot width of sidewalk

KEY (CORRECT ANSWERS)

1. A
2. C
3. B
4. C

TEST 4

Questions 1-6.

DIRECTIONS: Questions 1 through 6 are to be answered SOLELY on the basis of the information given in Figure I below.

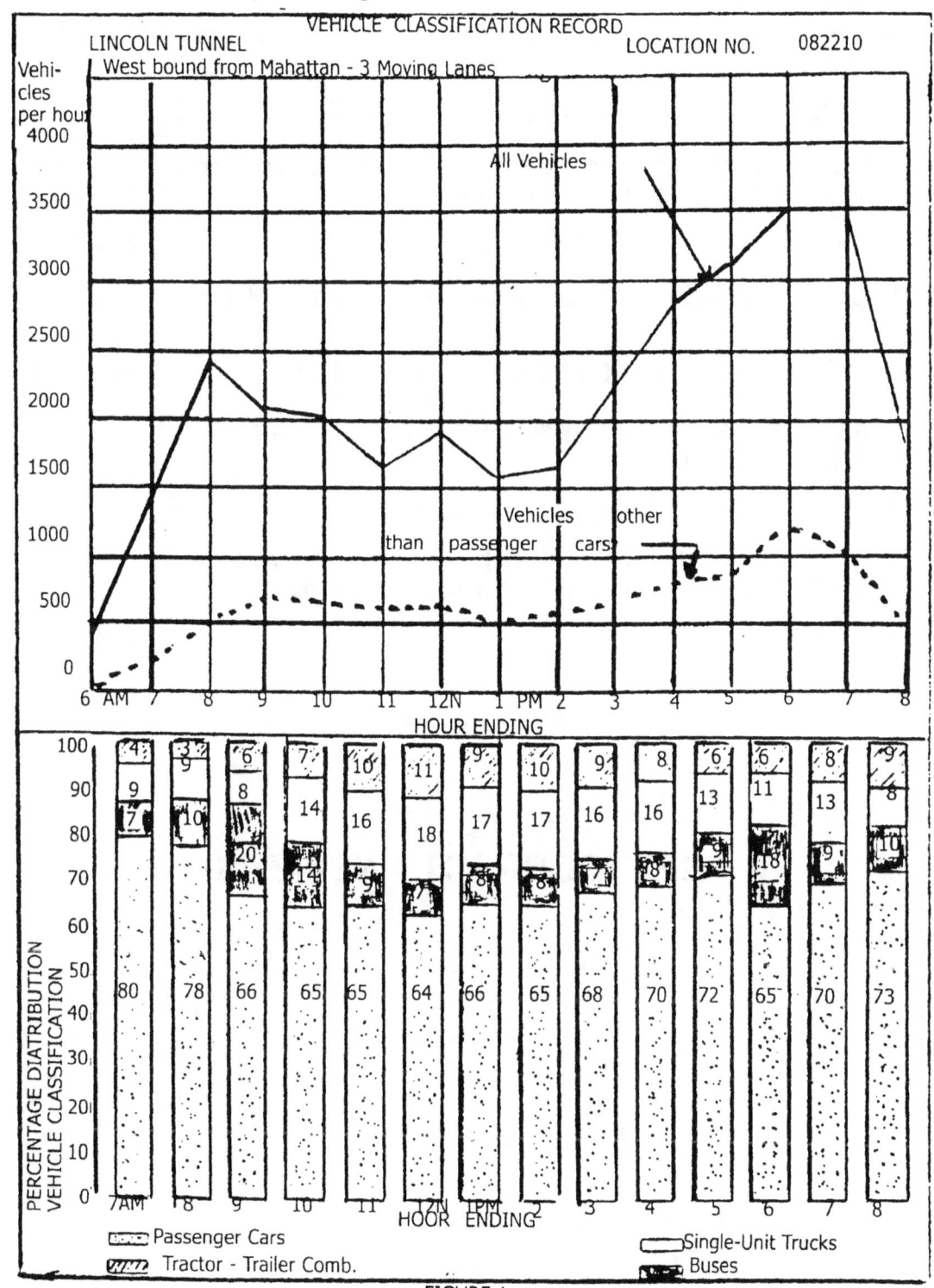

FIGURE 1

1. The total number of all vehicles traveling through the Lincoln Tunnel westbound from Manhattan between the hours of 6 A.M. and 12 Noon is MOST NEARLY

    A. 5,500   B. 7,500   C. 9,500   D. 11,500

2. The number of passenger cars recorded during the hour ending at 7 P.M. was MOST NEARLY

    A. 235   B. 1,160   C. 2,450   D. 3,500

3. Excluding passenger cars, the average number of vehicles per moving lane recorded during the peak hour was MOST NEARLY

    A. 420   B. 1,180   C. 1,250   D. 3,550

4. The percentage of buses recorded between 6 A.M. and 8 P.M. ranged between _____ and _____.

    A. 3%; 11%   B. 8%; 18%   C. 6%; 20%   D. 64%; 80%

5. During the study period, the percentage of single unit trucks EXCEEDED the percentage of buses for _____ hours.

    A. 4   B. 5   C. 9   D. 10

6. For all vehicles reported, the recorded traffic volume during the morning peak hour was MOST NEARLY _____ of the volume during the evening peak hour.

    A. 40%   B. 50%   C. 60%   D. 70%

KEY (CORRECT ANSWERS)

1. D
2. C
3. A
4. C
5. C
6. D

PREPARING WRITTEN MATERIAL

PARAGRAPH REARRANGEMENT
COMMENTARY

The sentences that follow are in scrambled order. You are to rearrange them in proper order and indicate the letter choice containing the correct answer at the space at the right.

Each group of sentences in this section is actually a paragraph presented in scrambled order. Each sentence in the group has a place in that paragraph; no sentence is to be left out. You are to read each group of sentences and decide upon the best order in which to put the sentences so as to form a well-organized paragraph.

The questions in this section measure the ability to solve a problem when all the facts relevant to its solution are not given.

More specifically, certain positions of responsibility and authority require the employee to discover connection between events sometimes, apparently, unrelated. In order to do this, the employee will find it necessary to correctly infer that unspecified events have probably occurred or are likely to occur. This ability becomes especially important when action must be taken on incomplete information.

Accordingly, these questions require competitors to choose among several suggested alternatives, each of which presents a different sequential arrangement of the events. Competitors must choose the MOST logical of the suggested sequences.

In order to do so, they may be required to draw on general knowledge to infer missing concepts or events that are essential to sequencing the given events. Competitors should be careful to infer only what is essential to the sequence. The plausibility of the wrong alternatives will always require the inclusion of unlikely events or of additional chains of events which are NOT essential to sequencing the given events.

It's very important to remember that you are looking for the best of the four possible choices, and that the best choice of all may not even be one of the answers you're given to choose from.

There is no one right way to solve these problems. Many people have found it helpful to first write out the order of the sentences, as they would have arranged them, on their scrap paper before looking at the possible answers. If their optimum answer is there, this can save them some time. If it isn't, this method can still give insight into solving the problem. Others find it most helpful to just go through each of the possible choices, contrasting each as they go along. You should use whatever method feels comfortable and works for you.

While most of these types of questions are not that difficult, we've added a higher percentage of the difficult type, just to give you more practice. Usually there are only one or two questions on this section that contain such subtle distinctions that you're unable to answer confidently. And you then may find yourself stuck deciding between two possible choices, neither of which you're sure about.

EXAMINATION SECTION
TEST 1

DIRECTIONS: The sentences that follow are in scrambled order. You are to rearrange them in proper order and indicate the letter choice containing the correct answer. *PRINT THE LETTER OF THE CORRECT ANSWER IN THE SPACE AT THE RIGHT.*

1. Below are four statements labeled W, X, Y and Z. 1.____
   W. He was a strict and fanatic drillmaster.
   X. The word is always used in a derogatory sense and generally shows resentment and anger on the part of the user.
   Y. It is from the name of this Frenchman that we derive our English word, martinet.
   Z. Jean Martinet was the Inspector-General of Infantry during the reign of King Louis XIV.
   The PROPER order in which these sentences should be placed in a paragraph is:
   A. X, Z, W, Y   B. X, Z, Y, W   C. Z, W, Y, X   D. Z, Y, W, X

2. In the following paragraph, the sentences, which are numbered, have been jumbled. 2.____
   I. Since then it has undergone changes.
   II. It was incorporated in 1955 under the laws of the State of New York.
   III. Its primary purposes, a cleaner city, has, however, remained the same.
   IV. The Citizens Committee works in cooperation with the Mayor's Inter-departmental Committee for a Clean City. 3.____
   The order in which these sentences should be arranged to form a well-organized paragraph is:
   A. II, IV, I, III   B. III, IV, I, II   C. IV, II, I, III   D. IV, III, II, I

Questions 3-5.

DIRECTIONS: The sentences listed below are part of a meaningful paragraph but they are not given in their proper order. You are to decide what would be the BEST order in which to put the sentences so as to form a well-organized paragraph. Each sentence has a place in the paragraph; there are no extra sentences. You are then to answer Questions 3 through 5 inclusive on the basis of your rearrangements of these scrambled sentences into a properly organized paragraph.

In 1887 some insurance companies organized an Inspection Department to advise their clients on all phases of fire prevention and protection. Probably this has been due to the smaller annual fire losses in Great Britain than in the United States. It tests various fire prevention devices and appliances and determines manufacturing hazards and their safeguards. Fire research began earlier in the United States and is more advanced than in Great Britain. Later they established a laboratory specializing in electrical, mechanical, hydraulic, and chemical fields.

2 (#1)

3. When the five sentences are arranged in proper order, the paragraph starts with the sentence which begins
   A. "In 1887…"
   B. "Probably this…"
   C. "It tests…"
   D. "Fire research…"
   E. "Later they…"

3._____

4. In the last sentence listed above, "they" refers to
   A. the insurance companies
   B. the United States and Great Britain
   C. the Inspection Department
   D. clients
   E. technicians

4._____

5. When the above paragraph is properly arranged, it ends with the words
   A. "…and protection."
   B. "…the United States."
   C. "…their safeguards."
   D. "…in Great Britain."
   E. "…chemical fields."

5._____

KEY (CORRECT ANSWERS)

1. C
2. C
3. D
4. A
5. C

TEST 2

DIRECTIONS: In each of the questions numbered I through V, several sentences are given. For each question, choose as your answer the group of number that represents the MOST logical order of these sentences if they were arranged in paragraph form. *PRINT THE LETTER OF THE CORRECT ANSWER IN THE SPACE AT THE RIGHT.*

1. I. It is established when one shows that the landlord has prevented the tenant's enjoyment of his interest in the property leased.
    II. Constructive eviction is the result of a breach of the covenant of quiet enjoyment implied in all leases.
    III. In some parts of the United States, it is not complete until the tenant vacates within a reasonable time.
    IV. Generally, the acts must be of such serious and permanent character as to deny the tenant the enjoyment of his possessing rights.
    V. In this event, upon abandonment of the premises, the tenant's liability for that ceases.
    The CORRECT answer is:
    A. II, I, IV, III, V
    B. V, II, III, I, IV
    C. IV, III, I, II, V
    D. I, III, V, IV, II

    1.____

2. I. The powerlessness before private and public authorities that is the typical experience of the slum tenant is reminiscent of the situation of blue-collar workers all through the nineteenth century.
    II. Similarly, in recent years, this chapter of history has been reopened by anti-poverty groups which have attempted to organize slum tenants to enable them to bargain collectively with their landlords about the conditions of their tenancies.
    III. It is familiar history that many of the worker remedied their condition by joining together and presenting their demands collectively.
    IV. Like the workers, tenants are forced by the conditions of modern life into substantial dependence on these who possess great political aid and economic power.
    V. What's more, the very fact of dependence coupled with an absence of education and self-confidence makes them hesitant and unable to stand up for what they need from those in power.
    The CORRECT answer is:
    A. V, IV, I, II, III
    B. II, III, I, V, IV
    C. III, I, V, IV, II
    D. I, IV, V, III, II

    2.____

3. I. A railroad, for example, when not acting as a common carrier may contract away responsibility for its own negligence.
    II. As to a landlord, however, no decision has been found relating to the legal effect of a clause shifting the statutory duty of repair to the tenant.
    III. The courts have not passed on the validity of clauses relieving the landlord of this duty and liability.
    IV. They have, however, upheld the validity of exculpatory clauses in other types of contracts.

    3.____

61

V. Housing regulations impose a duty upon the landlord to maintain leased premises in safe condition.
VI. As another example, a bailee may limit his liability except for gross negligence, willful acts, or fraud.

The CORRECT answer is:
A. II, I, VI, IV, III, V
B. I, III, IV, V, VI, II
C. III, V, I, IV, II, VI
D. V, III, IV, I, VI, II

4.
I. Since there are only samples in the building, retail or consumer sales are generally eschewed by mart occupants, and in some instances, rigid controls are maintained to limit entrance to the mart only to those persons engaged in retailing.
II. Since World War I, in many larger cities, there has developed a new type of property, called the mart building.
III. It can, therefore, be used by wholesalers and jobbers for the display of sample merchandise.
IV. This type of building is most frequently a multi-storied, finished interior property which is a cross between a retail arcade and a loft building.
V. This limitation enables the mart occupants to ship the orders from another location after the retailer or dealer makes his selection from the samples.

The CORRECT answer is:
A. II, IV, III, I, V
B. IV, III, V, I, II
C. I, III, II, IV, V
D. I, IV, II, III, V

5.
I. In general, staff-line friction reduces the distinctive contribution of staff personnel.
II. The conflicts, however, introduce an uncontrolled element into the managerial system.
III. On the other hand, the natural resistance of the line to staff innovations probably usefully restrains over-eager efforts to apply untested procedures on a large scale.
IV. Under such conditions, it is difficult to know when valuable ideas are being sacrificed.
V. The relatively weak position of staff, requiring accommodation to the line, tends to restrict their ability to engage in free, experimental innovation.

The CORRECT answer is:
A. IV, II, III, I, V
B. I, V, III, II, IV
C. V, III, I, II, IV
D. II, I, IV, V, III

KEY (CORRECT ANSWERS)

1. A
2. D
3. D
4. A
5. B

TEST 3

DIRECTIONS: Questions 1 through 4 consist of six sentences which can be arranged in a logical sequence. For each question, select the choice which places the numbered sentences in the MOST logical sequent. *PRINT THE LETTER OF THE CORRECT ANSWER IN THE SPACE AT THE RIGHT.*

1.
   I. The burden of proof as to each issue is determined before trial and remains upon the same party throughout the trial.
   II. The jury is at liberty to believe one witness' testimony as against a number of contradictory witnesses.
   III. In a civil case, the party bearing the burden of proof is required to prove his contention by a fair preponderance of the evidence.
   IV. However, it must be noted that a fair preponderance of evidence does not necessarily mean a greater number of witnesses.
   V. The burden of proof is the burden which rests upon one of the parties to an action to persuade the trier of the facts, generally the jury, that a proposition he asserts is true.
   VI. If the evidence is equally balanced, or if it leaves the jury in such doubt as to be unable to decide the controversy either way, judgment must be given against the party upon whom the burden of proof rests.
   The CORRECT answer is:
   A. III, II, V, IV, I, VI
   B. I, II, VI, V, III, IV
   C. III, IV, V, I, II, VI
   D. V, I, III, VI, IV, II

1.____

2.
   I. If a parent is without assets and is unemployed, he cannot be convicted of the crime of non-support of a child.
   II. The term "sufficient ability" has been held to mean sufficient financial ability.
   III. It does not matter if his unemployment is by choice or unavoidable circumstances.
   IV. If he fails to take any steps at all, he may be liable to prosecution for endangering the welfare of a child.
   V. Under the penal law, a parent is responsible for the support of his minor child only if the parent is "of sufficient ability."
   VI. An indigent parent may meet his obligation by borrowing money or by seeking aid under the provisions of the Social Welfare Law.
   The CORRECT answer is:
   A. VI, I, V, III, II, IV
   B. I, III, V, II, IV, VI
   C. V, II, I, III, VI, IV
   D. I, VI, IV, V, II, III

2.____

3.
   I. Consider, for example, the case of a rabble rouser who urges a group of twenty people to go out and break the windows of a nearby factory.
   II. Therefore, the law fills the indicated gap with the crime of inciting to riot.
   III. A person is considered guilty of inciting to riot when he urges ten or more persons to engage in tumultuous and violent conduct of a kind likely to create public alarm.
   IV. However, if he has not obtained the cooperation of at least four people, he cannot be charged with unlawful assembly.

3.____

63

V. The charge of inciting to riot was added to the law to cover types of conduct which cannot be classified as either the crime of "riot" or the crime of "unlawful assembly."
VI. If he acquires the acquiescence of at least four of them, he is guilty of unlawful assembly even if the project does not materialize.

The CORRECT answer is:
A. III, V, I, VI, IV, II
B. V, I, IV, VI, II, III
C. III, IV, I, V, II, VI
D. V, I, IV, VI, III, II

4. I. If, however, the rebuttal evidence presents an issue of credibility, it is for the jury to determine whether the presumption has, in fact, been destroyed.
    II. Once sufficient evidence to the contrary is introduced, the presumption disappears from the trial.
    III. The effect of a presumption is to place the burden upon the adversary to come forward with evidence to rebut the presumption.
    IV. When a presumption is overcome and ceases to exist in the case, the fact or facts which gave rise to the presumption still remain.
    V. Whether a presumption has been overcome is ordinarily a question for the court.
    VI. Such information may furnish a basis for a logical inference.

The CORRECT answer is:
A. IV, VI, II, V, I, III
B. III, II, V, I, IV, VI
C. V, III, VI, IV, II, I
D. V, IV, I, II, VI, III

KEY (CORRECT ANSWERS)

1. D
2. C
3. A
4. B

PREPARING WRITTEN MATERIAL
EXAMINATION SECTION
TEST 1

DIRECTIONS: Each of the sentences in this test may be classified under one of the following four categories:
- A. Faulty because of incorrect grammar or word usage
- B. Faulty because of incorrect punctuation
- C. Faulty because of incorrect capitalization or incorrect spelling
- D. Correct

Examine each sentence carefully to determine under which of the above four options it is best classified. Then, in the space to the right, print the capital letter preceding the option which is the BEST of the four suggested above. (Note that each faulty sentence contains but one type of error. Consider a sentence to be correct if it contains none of the types of errors mentioned, even though there may be other correct ways of expressing the same thought.)

1. He sent the notice to the clerk who you hired yesterday.   1.____

2. It must be admitted, however that you were not informed of this change.   2.____

3. Only the employee who have served in this grade for at least two years are eligible for promotion.   3.____

4. The work was divided equally between she and Mary.   4.____

5. He thought that you were not available at that time.   5.____

6. When the messenger returns; please give him this package.   6.____

7. The new secretary prepared, typed, addressed, and delivered, the notices.   7.____

8. Walking into the room, his desk can be seen at the rear.   8.____

9. Although John has worked here longer than She, he produces a smaller amount of work.   9.____

10. She said she could of typed this report yesterday.   10.____

11. Neither one of these procedures are adequate for the efficient performance of this task.   11.____

12. The typewriter is the tool of the typist; the cash register, the tool of the cashier.   12.____

13. "The assignment must be completed as soon as possible" said the supervisor.   13.____

14. As you know, office handbooks are issued to all new Employees.   14.____

15. Writing a speech is sometimes easier than to deliver it before an audience.   15.____

16. Mr. Brown our accountant, will audit the accounts next week.   16.____

17. Give the assignment to whomever is able to do it most efficiently.   17.____

18. The supervisor expected either your or I to file these reports.   18.____

KEY (CORRECT ANSWERS)

1.	A	11.	A
2.	B	12.	C
3.	D	13.	B
4.	A	14.	C
5.	D	15.	A
6.	B	16.	B
7.	B	17.	A
8.	A	18.	A
9.	C		
10.	A		

TEST 2

DIRECTIONS: Each of the sentences in this test may be classified under one of the following four categories:
A. Faulty because of incorrect grammar or word usage
B. Faulty because of incorrect punctuation
C. Faulty because of incorrect capitalization or incorrect spelling
D. Correct

Examine each sentence carefully to determine under which of the above four options it is best classified. Then, in the space to the right, print the capital letter preceding the option which is the BEST of the four suggested above. (Note that each faulty sentence contains but one type of error. Consider a sentence to be correct if it contains none of the types of errors mentioned, even though there may be other correct ways of expressing the same thought.)

1. The fire apparently started in the storeroom, which is usually locked.   1._____
2. On approaching the victim, two bruises were noticed by this officer.   2._____
3. The officer, who was there examined the report with great care.   3._____
4. Each employee in the office had a seperate desk.   4._____
5. All employees including members of the clerical staff, were invited to the lecture.   5._____
6. The suggested Procedure is similar to the one now in use.   6._____
7. No one was more pleased with the new procedure than the chauffeur.   7._____
8. He tried to persaude her to change the procedure.   8._____
9. The total of the expenses charged to petty cash were high.   9._____
10. An understanding between him and I was finally reached.   10._____

KEY (CORRECT ANSWERS)

1.	D	6.	C
2.	A	7.	D
3.	B	8.	C
4.	C	9.	A
5.	B	10.	A

TEST 3

DIRECTIONS: Each of the sentences in this test may be classified under one of the following four categories:
    A. Faulty because of incorrect grammar or word usage
    B. Faulty because of incorrect punctuation
    C. Faulty because of incorrect capitalization or incorrect spelling
    D. Correct

Examine each sentence carefully to determine under which of the above four options it is best classified. Then, in the space to the right, print the capital letter preceding the option which is the BEST of the four suggested above. (Note that each faulty sentence contains but one type of error. Consider a sentence to be correct if it contains none of the types of errors mentioned, even though there may be other correct ways of expressing the same thought.)

1. They told both he and I that the prisoner had escaped. 1.____

2. Any superior officer, who, disregards the just complaint of his subordinates, is remiss in the performance of his duty. 2.____

3. Only those members of the national organization who resided in the Middle West attended the conference in Chicago. 3.____

4. We told him to give the national organization assignment to whoever was available. 4.____

5. Please do not disappoint and embarass us by not appearing in court. 5.____

6. Although the office's speech proved to be entertaining, the topic was not relevent to the main theme of the conference. 6.____

7. In February all new officers attended a training course in which they were learned in their principal duties and the fundamental operating procedure of the department. 7.____

8. I personally seen inmate Jones threaten inmates Smith and Green with bodily harm if they refused to participate in the plot. 8.____

9. To the layman, who on a chance visit to the prison observes everything functioning smoothly, the maintenance of prison discipline may seem to be a relatively easily realizable objective. 9.____

10. The prisoners in cell block fourty were forbidden to sit on the cell cots during the recreation hour. 10.____

KEY (CORRECT ANSWERS)

1.	A	6.	C
2.	B	7.	A
3.	C	8.	A
4.	D	9.	D
5.	C	10.	C

TEST 4

DIRECTIONS: Each of the sentences in this test may be classified under one of the following four categories:
- A. Faulty because of incorrect grammar or word usage
- B. Faulty because of incorrect punctuation
- C. Faulty because of incorrect capitalization or incorrect spelling
- D. Correct

Examine each sentence carefully to determine under which of the above four options it is best classified. Then, in the space to the right, print the capital letter preceding the option which is the BEST of the four suggested above. (Note that each faulty sentence contains but one type of error. Consider a sentence to be correct if it contains none of the types of errors mentioned, even though there may be other correct ways of expressing the same thought.)

1. I cannot encourage you any.   1.____
2. You always look well in those sort of clothes.   2.____
3. Shall we go to the park?   3.____
4. The man whome he introduced was Mr. Carey.   4.____
5. She saw the letter laying here this morning.   5.____
6. It should rain before the Afternoon is over.   6.____
7. They have already went home.   7.____
8. That Jackson will be elected is evident.   8.____
9. He does not hardly approve of us.   9.____
10. It was he, who won the prize.   10.____

KEY (CORRECT ANSWERS)

1.	A	6.	C
2.	A	7.	A
3.	D	8.	D
4.	C	9.	A
5.	A	10.	B

TEST 5

DIRECTIONS: Each of the sentences in this test may be classified under one of the following four categories:
- A. Faulty because of incorrect grammar or word usage
- B. Faulty because of incorrect punctuation
- C. Faulty because of incorrect capitalization or incorrect spelling
- D. Correct

Examine each sentence carefully to determine under which of the above four options it is best classified. Then, in the space to the right, print the capital letter preceding the option which is the BEST of the four suggested above. (Note that each faulty sentence contains but one type of error. Consider a sentence to be correct if it contains none of the types of errors mentioned, even though there may be other correct ways of expressing the same thought.)

1. Shall we go to the park. 1.____
2. They are, alike, in this particular way. 2.____
3. They gave the poor man sume food when he knocked on the door. 3.____
4. I regret the loss caused by the error. 4.____
5. The students' will have a new teacher. 5.____
6. They sweared to bring out all the facts. 6.____
7. He decided to open a branch store on 33rd street. 7.____
8. His speed is equal and more than that of a racehorse. 8.____
9. He felt very warm on that Summer day. 9.____
10. He was assisted by his friend, who lives in the next house. 10.____

KEY (CORRECT ANSWERS)

1.	B	6.	A
2.	B	7.	C
3.	C	8.	A
4.	D	9.	C
5.	B	10.	D

TEST 6

DIRECTIONS: Each of the sentences in this test may be classified under one of the following four categories:
- A. Faulty because of incorrect grammar or word usage
- B. Faulty because of incorrect punctuation
- C. Faulty because of incorrect capitalization or incorrect spelling
- D. Correct

Examine each sentence carefully to determine under which of the above four options it is best classified. Then, in the space to the right, print the capital letter preceding the option which is the BEST of the four suggested above. (Note that each faulty sentence contains but one type of error. Consider a sentence to be correct if it contains none of the types of errors mentioned, even though there may be other correct ways of expressing the same thought.)

1. The climate of New York is colder than California.   1.____
2. I shall wait for you on the corner.   2.____
3. Did we see the boy who, we think, is the leader.   3.____
4. Being a modest person, John seldom talks about his invention.   4.____
5. The gang is called the smith street bos.   5.____
6. He seen the man break into the store.   6.____
7. We expected to lay still there for quite a while.   7.____
8. He is considered to be the Leader of his organization.   8.____
9. Although I recieved an invitation, I won't go.   9.____
10. The letter must be here some place.   10.____

KEY (CORRECT ANSWERS)

1.	A		6.	A
2.	D		7.	A
3.	B		8.	C
4.	D		9.	C
5.	C		10.	A

TEST 7

DIRECTIONS: Each of the sentences in this test may be classified under one of the following four categories:
- A. Faulty because of incorrect grammar or word usage
- B. Faulty because of incorrect punctuation
- C. Faulty because of incorrect capitalization or incorrect spelling
- D. Correct

Examine each sentence carefully to determine under which of the above four options it is best classified. Then, in the space to the right, print the capital letter preceding the option which is the BEST of the four suggested above. (Note that each faulty sentence contains but one type of error. Consider a sentence to be correct if it contains none of the types of errors mentioned, even though there may be other correct ways of expressing the same thought.)

1. I though it to be he.   1.____
2. We expect to remain here for a long time.   2.____
3. The committee was agreed.   3.____
4. Two-thirds of the building are finished.   4.____
5. The water was froze.   5.____
6. Everyone of the salesmen must supply their own car.   6.____
7. Who is the author of Gone With the Wind?   7.____
8. He marched on and declaring that he would never surrender.   8.____
9. Who shall I say called?   9.____
10. Everyone has left but they.   10.____

KEY (CORRECT ANSWERS)

1.	A	6.	A
2.	D	7.	B
3.	D	8.	A
4.	A	9.	D
5.	A	10.	D

TEST 8

DIRECTIONS: Each of the sentences in this test may be classified under one of the following four categories:
- A. Faulty because of incorrect grammar or word usage
- B. Faulty because of incorrect punctuation
- C. Faulty because of incorrect capitalization or incorrect spelling
- D. Correct

Examine each sentence carefully to determine under which of the above four options it is best classified. Then, in the space to the right, print the capital letter preceding the option which is the BEST of the four suggested above. (Note that each faulty sentence contains but one type of error. Consider a sentence to be correct if it contains none of the types of errors mentioned, even though there may be other correct ways of expressing the same thought.)

1. Who did we give the order to?
2. Send your order in immediately.
3. I believe I paid the Bill.
4. I have not met but one person.
5. Why aren't Tom, and Fred, going to the dance?
6. What reason is there for him not going?
7. The seige of Malta was a tremendous event.
8. I was there yesterday I assure you
9. Your ukulele is better than mine.
10. No one was there only Mary.

KEY (CORRECT ANSWERS)

1. A
2. D
3. C
4. A
5. B
6. A
7. C
8. B
9. C
10. A

TEST 9

DIRECTIONS: In each of the following groups of sentences, one of the four sentences is faulty in grammar, punctuation, or capitalization. Select the INCORRECT sentence in each case.

1. A. If you had stood at home and done your homework, you would not have failed in arithmetic.
   B. Her affected manner annoyed every member of the audience.
   C. How will the new law affect our income taxes?
   D. The plants were not affected by the long, cold winter, but they succumbed to the drought of summer.

   1._____

2. A. He is one of the most able men who have been in the Senate.
   B. It is he who is to blame for the lamentable mistake.
   C. Haven't you a helpful suggestion to make at this time?
   D. The money was robbed from the blind man's cup.

   2._____

3. A. The amount of children in this school is steadily increasing.
   B. After taking an apple from the table, she went out to play.
   C. He borrowed a dollar from me.
   D. I had hoped my brother would arrive before me.

   3._____

4. A. Whom do you think I hear from every week?
   B. Who do you think is the right man for the job?
   C. Who do you think I found in the room?
   D. He is the man whom we considered a good candidate for the presidency.

   4._____

5. A. Quietly the puppy laid down before the fireplace.
   B. You have made your bed; now lie in it.
   C. I was badly sunburned because I had lain too long in the sun.
   D. I laid the doll on the bed and left the room.

   5._____

KEY (CORRECT ANSWERS)

1. A
2. D
3. A
4. C
5. A

REPORT WRITING

EXAMINATION SECTION

TEST 1

DIRECTIONS: Each question or incomplete statement is followed by several suggested answers or completions. Select the one that BEST answers the question or completes the statement. *PRINT THE LETTER OF THE CORRECT ANSWER IN THE SPACE AT THE RIGHT.*

Questions 1-4.

DIRECTIONS: Answer Questions 1 through 4 on the basis of the following report which was prepared by a supervisor for inclusion in his agency's annual report.

Line #
1   On Oct. 13, I was assigned to study the salaries paid.
2   to clerical employees in various titles by the city and by
3   private industry in the area.
4   In order to get the data I needed, I called Mr. Johnson at
5   the Bureau of the Budget and the payroll officers at X Corp.—
6   a brokerage house, Y Co. —an insurance company, and Z Inc. —
7   a publishing firm. None of them was available and I had to call
8   all of them again the next day.
9   When I finally got the information I needed, I drew up a
10 chart, which is attached. Note that not all of the companies I
11 contacted employed people at all the different levels used in the
12 city service.
13 The conclusions I draw from analyzing this information is
14 as follows: The city's entry-level salary is about average for
15 the region; middle-level salaries are generally higher in the
16 city government plan than in private industry; but salaries at the
17 highest levels in private industry are better than city em-
18 ployees' pay.

1. Which of the following criticisms about the style in which this report is written is MOST valid?
   A. It is too informal.
   B. It is too concise.
   C. It is too choppy.
   D. The syntax is too complex.

   1._____

2. Judging from the statements made in the report, the method followed by this employee in performing his research was
   A. *good*; he contacted a representative sample of businesses in the area
   B. *poor*; he should have drawn more definite conclusions
   C. *good*; he was persistent in collecting information
   D. *poor*; he did not make a thorough study

   2._____

3. One sentence in this report contains a grammatical error. This sentence begins on line number
   A. 4   B. 7   C. 10   D. 14

4. The type of information given in this report which should be presented in footnotes or in an appendix is the
   A. purpose of the study
   B. specifics about the businesses contacted
   C. reference to the chart
   D. conclusions drawn by the author

5. The use of a graph to show statistical data in a report is SUPERIOR to a table because it
   A. features approximations
   B. emphasizes facts and relationships more dramatically
   C. presents data more accurately
   D. is easily understood by the average reader

6. Of the following, the degree of formality required of a written report in tone is MOST likely to depend on the
   A. subject matter of the report
   B. frequency of its occurrence
   C. amount of time available for its preparation
   D. audience for whom the report is intended

7. Of the following, a distinguishing characteristic of a written report intended for the head of your agency as compared to a report prepared for a lower-echelon staff member is that the report for the agency head should USUALLY include
   A. considerably more detail, especially statistical data
   B. the essential details in an abbreviated form
   C. all available source material
   D. an annotated bibliography

8. Assume that you are asked to write a lengthy report for use by the administrator of your agency, the subject of which is "The Impact of Proposed New Data Processing Operation on Line Personnel" in your agency. You decide that the *most* appropriate type of report for you to prepare is an analytical report, including recommendations.
   The MAIN reason for your decision is that
   A. the subject of the report is extremely complex
   B. large sums of money are involved
   C. the report is being prepared for the administrator
   D. you intend to include charts and graphs

9. Assume that you are preparing a report based on a survey dealing with the attitudes of employees in Division X regarding proposed new changes in compensating employees for working overtime. Three percent of the respondents to the survey voluntarily offer an unfavorable opinion on the method of assigning overtime work, a question not specifically asked of the employees.
   On the basis of this information, the MOST appropriate and significant of the following comments for you to make in the report with regard to employees' attitudes on assigning overtime work is that
   A. an insignificant percentage of employees dislike the method of assigning overtime work
   B. three percent of the employees in Division X dislike the method of assigning overtime work
   C. three percent of the sample selected for the survey voiced an unfavorable opinion on the method of assigning overtime work
   D. some employees voluntarily voiced negative feelings about the method of assigning overtime work, making it impossible to determine the extent of this attitude

10. A supervisor should be able to prepare a report that is well-written and unambiguous.
    Of the following sentences that might appear in a report, select the one which communicates MOST clearly the intent of its author.
    A. When your subordinates speak to a group of people, they should be well-informed.
    B. When he asked him to leave, SanMan King told him that he would refuse the request.
    C. Because he is a good worker, Foreman Jefferson assigned Assistant Foreman D'Agostino to replace him.
    D. Each of us is responsible for the actions of our subordinates.

11. In some reports, especially longer ones, a list of the resources (books, papers, magazines, etc.) used to prepare it is included. This list is called the
    A. accreditation B. bibliography
    C. summary   D. glossary

12. Reports are usually divided into several sections, some of which are more necessary than others.
    Of the following, the section which is ABSOLUTELY necessary to include in a report is
    A. a table of contents B. the body
    C. an index   D. a bibliography

13. Suppose you are writing a report on an interview you have just completed with a particularly hostile applicant.
    Which of the following BEST describes what you should include in this report?
    A. What you think caused the applicant's hostile attitude during the interview
    B. Specific examples of the applicant's hostile remarks and behavior
    C. The relevant information uncovered during the interview
    D. A recommendation that the applicant's request be denied because of his hostility

14. When including recommendations in a report to your supervisor, which of the following is MOST important for you to do?
    A. Provide several alternative courses of action for each recommendation
    B. First present the supporting evidence, then the recommendations
    C. First present the recommendations, then the supporting evidence
    D. Make sure the recommendations arise logically out of the information in the report

15. It is often necessary that the writer of a report present facts and sufficient arguments to gain acceptance of the points, conclusions, or recommendations set forth in the report.
    Of the following, the LEAST advisable step to take in organizing a report, when such argumentation is the important factor, is a(n)
    A. elaborate expression of personal belief
    B. businesslike discussion of the problem as a whole
    C. orderly arrangement of convincing data
    D. reasonable explanation of the primary issues

16. In some types of reports, visual aids add interest, meaning, and support. They also provide an essential means of effectively communicating the message of the report.
    Of the following, the selection of the suitable visual aids to use with a report is LEAST dependent on the
    A. nature and scope of the report
    B. way in which the aid is to be used
    C. aid used in other reports
    D. prospective readers of the report

17. Visual aids used in a report may be placed either in the text material or in the appendix.
    Deciding where to put a chart, table, or any such aid should depend on the
    A. title of the report   B. purpose of the visual aid
    C. title of the visual aid   D. length of the report

18. A report is often revised several times before final preparation and distribution in an effort to make certain the report meets the needs of the situation for which it is designed.
    Which of the following is the BEST way for the author to be sure that a report covers the areas he intended?

A. Obtain a coworker's opinion
B. Compare it with a content checklist
C. Test it on a subordinate
D. Check his bibliography

19. In which of the following situations is an oral report preferable to a written report? When a(n)
   A. recommendation is being made for a future plan of action
   B. department head requests immediate information
   C. long-standing policy change is made
   D. analysis of complicated statistical data is involved

20. When an applicant is approved, the supervisor must fill in standard forms with certain information.
   The GREATEST advantage of using standard forms in this situation rather than having the supervisor write the report as he sees fit is that
   A. the report can be acted on quickly
   B. the report can be written without directions from a supervisor
   C. needed information is less likely to be left out of the report
   D. information that is written up this way is more likely to be verified

21. Assume that it is part of your job to prepare a monthly report for your unit head that eventually goes to the director. The report contains information on the number of applicants you have interviewed that have been approved and the number of applicants you have interviewed that have been turned down.
   Errors on such reports are serious because
   A. you are expected to be able to prove how many applicants you have interviewed each month
   B. accurate statistics are needed for effective management of the department
   C. they may not be discovered before the report is transmitted to the director
   D. they may result in loss to the applicants left out of the report

22. The frequency with which job reports are submitted should depend MAINLY on
   A. how comprehensive the report has to be
   B. the amount of information in the report
   C. the availability of an experienced man to write the report
   D. the importance of changes in the information included in the report

23. The CHIEF purpose in preparing an outline for a report is usually to insure that
   A. the report will be grammatically correct
   B. every point will be given equal emphasis
   C. principal and secondary points will be properly integrated
   D. the language of the report will be of the same level and include the same technical terms

24. The MAIN reason for requiring written job reports is to 24.____
    A. avoid the necessity of oral orders
    B. develop better methods of doing the work
    C. provide a permanent record of what was done
    D. increase the amount of work that can be done

25. Assume you are recommending in a report to your supervisor that a radical 25.____
    change in a standard maintenance procedure should be adopted.
    Of the following, the MOST important information to be included in this report is
    A. a list of the reasons for making this change
    B. the names of others who favor the change
    C. a complete description of the present procedure
    D. amount of training time needed for the new procedure

KEY (CORRECT ANSWERS)

1.	A	11.	B
2.	D	12.	B
3.	D	13.	C
4.	B	14.	D
5.	B	15.	A
6.	D	16.	C
7.	B	17.	B
8.	A	18.	B
9.	D	19.	B
10.	D	20.	C

21.	B
22.	D
23.	C
24.	C
25.	A

TEST 2

DIRECTIONS: Each question or incomplete statement is followed by several suggested answers or completions. Select the one that BEST answers the question or completes the statement. *PRINT THE LETTER OF THE CORRECT ANSWER IN THE SPACE AT THE RIGHT.*

1. It is often necessary that the writer of a report present facts and sufficient arguments to gain acceptance of the points, conclusions, or recommendations set forth in the report.
   Of the following, the LEAST advisable step to take in organizing a report, when such argumentation is the important factor, is a(n)
   A. elaborate expression of personal belief
   B. businesslike discussion of the problem as a whole
   C. orderly arrangement of convincing data
   D. reasonable explanation of the primary issues

   1.____

2. Of the following, the factor which is generally considered to be LEAST characteristic of a good control report is that it
   A. stresses performance that adheres to standard rather than emphasizing the exception
   B. supplies information intended to serve as the basis for corrective action
   C. provides feedback for the planning process
   D. includes data that reflect trends as well as current status

   2.____

3. An administrative assistant has been asked by his superior to write a concise, factual report with objective conclusions and recommendations based on facts assembled by other researchers.
   Of the following factors, the administrative assistant should give LEAST consideration to
   A. the educational level of the person or persons for whom the report is being prepared
   B. the use to be made of the report
   C. the complexity of the problem
   D. his own feelings about the importance of the problem

   3.____

4. When making a written report, it is often recommended that the findings or conclusions be presented near the beginning of the report.
   Of the following, the MOST important reason for doing this is that it
   A. facilitates organizing the material clearly
   B. assures that all the topics will be covered
   C. avoids unnecessary repetition of ideas
   D. prepares the reader for the facts that will follow

   4.____

5. You have been asked to write a report on methods of hiring and training new employees. Your report is going to be about ten pages long.
   For the convenience of your readers, a brief summary of your findings should
   A. appear at the beginning of your report
   B. be appended to the report as a postscript
   C. be circulated in a separate memo
   D. be inserted in tabular form in the middle of your report

6. In preparing a report, the MAIN reason for writing an outline is usually to
   A. help organize thoughts in a logical sequence
   B. provide a guide for the typing of the report
   C. allow the ultimate user to review the report in advance
   D. ensure that the report is being prepared on schedule

7. The one of the following which is MOST appropriate as a reason for including footnotes in a report is to
   A. correct capitalization
   B. delete passages
   C. improve punctuation
   D. cite references

8. A completed formal report may contain all of the following EXCEPT
   A. a synopsis
   B. a preface
   C. marginal notes
   D. bibliographical references

9. Of the following, the MAIN use of proofreaders' marks is to
   A. explain corrections to be made
   B. indicate that a manuscript has been read and approved
   C. let the reader know who proofread the report
   D. indicate the format of the report

10. Informative, readable, and concise reports have been found to observe the following rules:
    Rule I.   Keep the report short and easy to understand
    Rule II. Vary the length of sentences.
    Rule III. Vary the style of sentences so that, for example, they are not all just subject-verb, subject-verb.
    Consider this hospital laboratory report: The experiment was started in January. The apparatus was put together in six weeks. At that time, the synthesizing process was begun. The synthetic chemicals were separated. Then they were used in tests on patients.
    Which one of the following choices MOST accurately classifies the above rules into those which are violated by this report ad those which are not?
    A. II is violated, but I and III are not.
    B. III is violated, but I and II are not.
    C. II and III are violated, but I is not.
    D. I, II, and III are violated,

Questions 11-13.

DIRECTIONS: Questions 11 through 13 are based on the following example of a report. The report consists of eight numbered sentences, some of which are not consistent with the principles of good report writing.

(1) I interviewed Mrs. Loretta Crawford in Room 424 of County Hospital. (2) She had collapsed on the street and been brought into emergency. (3) She is an attractive woman with many friends judging by the cards she had received. (4) She did not know what her husband's last job had been, or what their present income was. (5) The first thing that Mrs. Crawford said was that she had never worked and that her husband was presently unemployed. (6) She did not know if they had any medical coverage or if they could pay the bill. (7) She said that her husband could not be reached by telephone but that he would be in to see her that afternoon. (8) I left word at the nursing station to be called when he arrived.

11. A good report should be arranged in logical order.
    Which of the following sentences from the report does NOT appear in its proper sequence in the report?
    A. 1   B. 4   C. 7   D. 8

12. Only material that is relevant to the main thought of a report should be included.
    Which of the following sentences from the report contains material which is LEAST relevant to this report? Sentence
    A. 3   B. 4   C. 6   D. 8

13. Reports should include all essential information.
    Of the following, the MOST important fact that is missing from this report is:
    A. Who was involved in the interview
    B. What was discovered at the interview
    C. When the interview took place
    D. Where the interview took place

Questions 14-15.

DIRECTIONS: Each of Questions 14 and 15 consists of four numbered sentences which constitute a paragraph in a report. They are not in the right order. Choose the numbered arrangement appearing after letter A, B, C, or D which is MOST logical and which BEST expresses the thought of the paragraph.

14. I. Congress made the commitment explicit in the Housing Act of 1949, establishing as a national goal the realization of a decent home and suitable environment for every American family.
    II. The result has been that the goal of decent home and suitable environment is still as far distant as ever for the disadvantaged urban family
    III. In spite of this action by Congress, federal housing programs have continued to be fragmented and grossly under-funded.
    IV. The passage of the National Housing Act signaled a new federal commitment to provide housing for the nation's citizens.

The CORRECT answer is:
A. I, IV, III, II   B. IV, I, III, II   C. IV, I, III, II   D. II, IV, I, III

15. I. The greater expense does not necessarily involve "exploitation," but it is often perceived as exploitative and unfair by those who are aware of the price differences involved, but unaware of operating costs.
    II. Ghetto residents believe they are "exploited" by local merchants, and evidence substantiates some of these beliefs.
    III. However, stores in low-income areas were more likely to be small independents, which could not achieve the economies available to supermarket chains and were, therefore, more likely to charge higher prices, and the customers were more likely to buy smaller-sized packages which are more expensive per unit of measure.
    IV. A study conducted in one city showed that distinctly higher prices were charged for goods sold in ghetto stores than in other areas.

    The CORRECT answer is:
    A. IV, II, I, III   B. IV, I, III, II   C. II, IV, III, I   D. II, III, IV, I

16. In organizing data to be presented in a formal report, the FIRST of the following steps should be
    A. determining the conclusions to be drawn
    B. establishing the time sequence of the data
    C. sorting and arranging like data into groups
    D. evaluating how consistently the data support the recommendations

17. All reports should be prepared with at least one copy so that
    A. there is one copy for your file
    B. there is a copy for your supervisor
    C. the report can be sent to more than one person
    D. the person getting the report can forward a copy to someone else

18. Before turning in a report of an investigation he has made, a supervisor discovers some additional information he did not include in this report. Whether he rewrites this report to include this additional information should PRIMARILY depend on the
    A. importance of the report itself
    B. number of people who will eventually review this report
    C. established policy covering the subject matter of the report
    D. bearing this new information has on the conclusions of the report

5 (#2)

KEY (CORRECT ANSWERS)

1.	A	11.	B
2.	A	12.	A
3.	D	13.	C
4.	D	14.	B
5.	A	15.	C
6.	A	16.	C
7.	D	17.	A
8.	C	18.	D
9.	A		
10.	C		

TRAFFIC ENGINEERING

BASIC FUNDAMENTALS OF TRAFFIC PLANNING

CONTENTS

	Page
CHAPTER 1 – CONCEPT	1-1
CHAPTER 2 – ORGANIZATION	2-1
CHAPTER 3 – PROCESS	3-1

Basic Fundamentals of Traffic Planning

THOROUGHFARE PLANNING *is a method of identifying travel needs and filling them — to make road travel safe, economical, convenient, free-flowing, and environmentally acceptable.* Thoroughfare planners insure that roadways will accommodate traffic demands, maximize the use of roadways, and solve traffic problems.

THOROUGHFARE PLANNING *provides not only for modifications to existing roadways to meet current traffic demands; it provides also for the identification of land areas that should be reserved for roadway expansion to meet future traffic demands.* Planners, working toward established goals, may recommend that a particular street be retained or redesigned as necessary to perform a specific function. **Effective thoroughfare planning can reap savings in construction and maintenance costs, protect housing areas, and control travel and land-use patterns.**

CONCEPT

PLANNING IS A STEP-BY-STEP PROCESS

The **planning process** is a method to:

Identify problems and establish goals and objectives.

Conduct traffic surveys, analyze the survey data, and estimate future traffic volumes and patterns.

Develop alternate solutions and test them against the goals and objectives, then select and implement a final plan.

Review and evaluate the plan on a continuing basis and adjust it as necessary to attain desired goals and objectives.

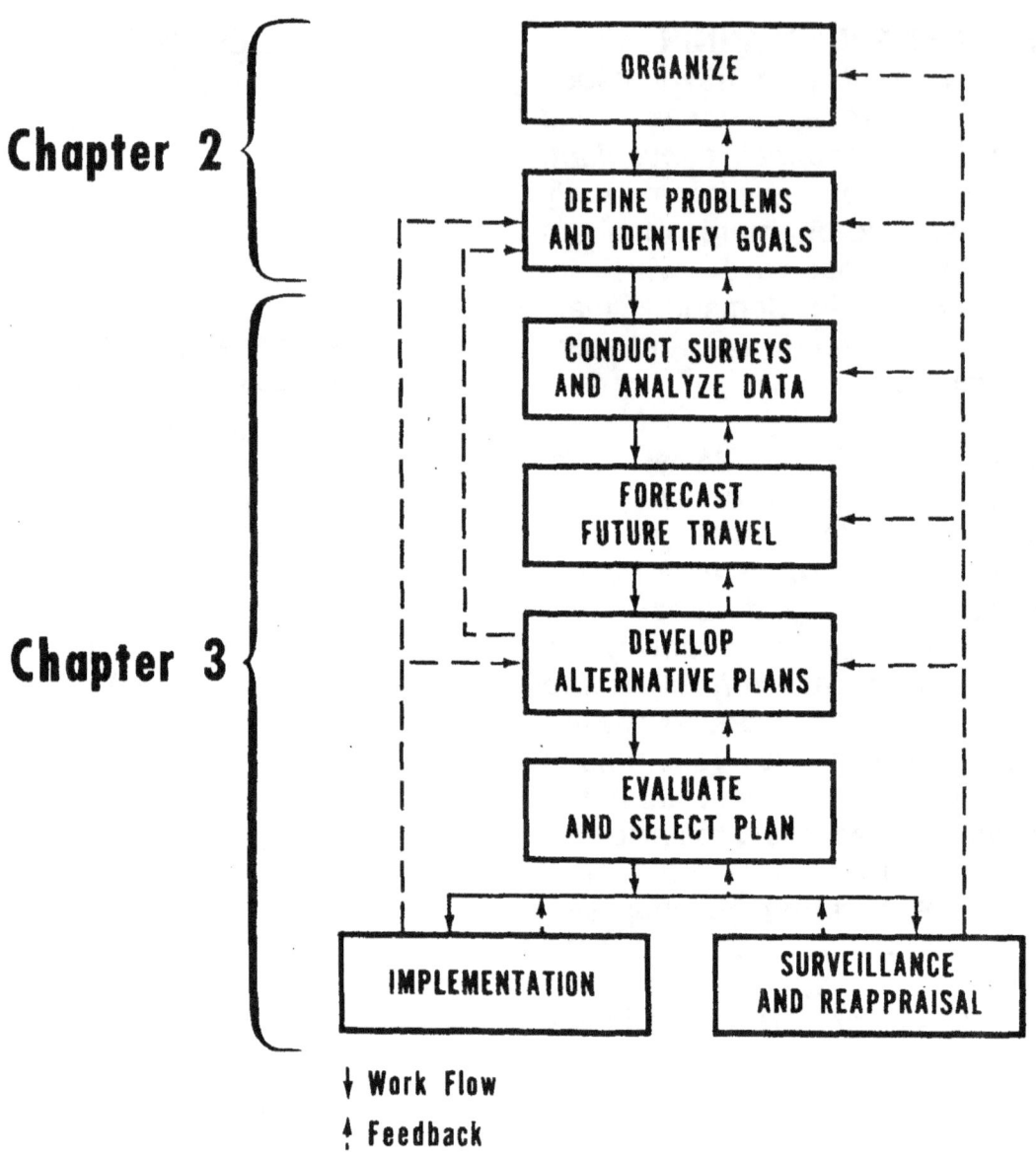

A step-by-step discussion of the planning process is presented in Chapters 2 and 3. Chapter 2 discusses the prerequisites to effective and continuing planning — that is, the formation of a planning committee, the identification of problems, and the establishment of goals. Chapter 3 summarizes the remaining steps to be taken to develop alternative plans for evaluation, selection, and implementation.

2-1

ORGANIZATION

PLANNING COMMITTEE

PROBLEM DEFINITION AND GOAL IDENTIFICATION

TRAFFIC PLANNING GOALS must be **determined by the installation decisionmakers,** with the **assistance of technical experts.** Technical experts should provide direction for the decisionmakers *through rational analysis of installation needs and policies.* With this information, **decisionmakers** can effectively select goals and a planning program that will insure an end product that is both workable and desirable.

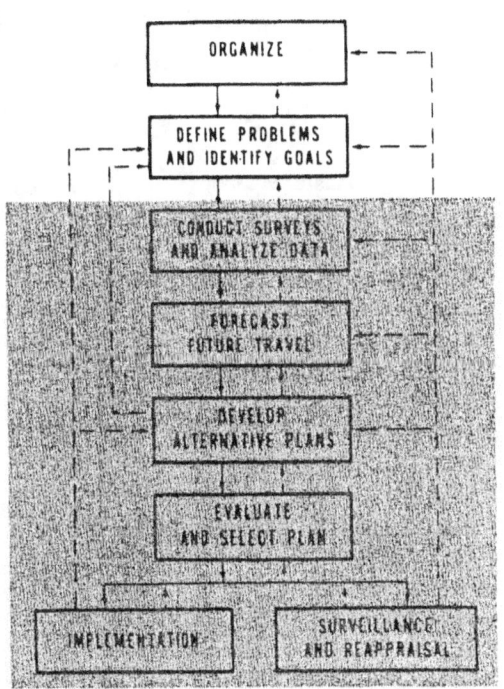

PLANNING COMMITTEE

EFFECTIVE THOROUGHFARE PLANNING *requires concerted effort among policymakers and the technical and administrative staffs of the installation under study.* Each step of the planning process must be based on a simple framework in which the installation's decisionmakers can clearly understand not only the traffic problems, but also the solution to those problems. Committee members usually should be selected to represent the installation's diverse disciplines and viewpoints. For example, an individual representing each of the groups shown below would be desirable.

DECISIONMAKERS MUST

- Identify Traffic Problems
- Establish Goals to Reduce Problems
- Select Thoroughfare Plan
- Gain Support for Plan

TECHNICAL STAFF MUST

- Conduct Traffic Studies
- Estimate Future Travel
- Develop Alternate Plans
- Implement Plan

PROBLEM DEFINITION AND GOAL IDENTIFICATION

THE FIRST STEP IN THOROUGHFARE PLANNING is to **clearly identify all traffic problems of the installation** being studied.

The term *"traffic problem"* is defined as *any situation that impairs the safe and efficient flow of traffic.*

In identifying traffic problems, relativity must be considered; that is, traffic problems vary among different areas of the country. For example, a 5-minute delay in New York City is considered as negligible, while the same delay in Timbuktu would be extremely frustrating to motorists. Therefore, it must be remembered that **traffic problems are relative to the installation being studied.**

FOR EVERY TRAFFIC PROBLEM, THERE IS A POSITIVE GOAL

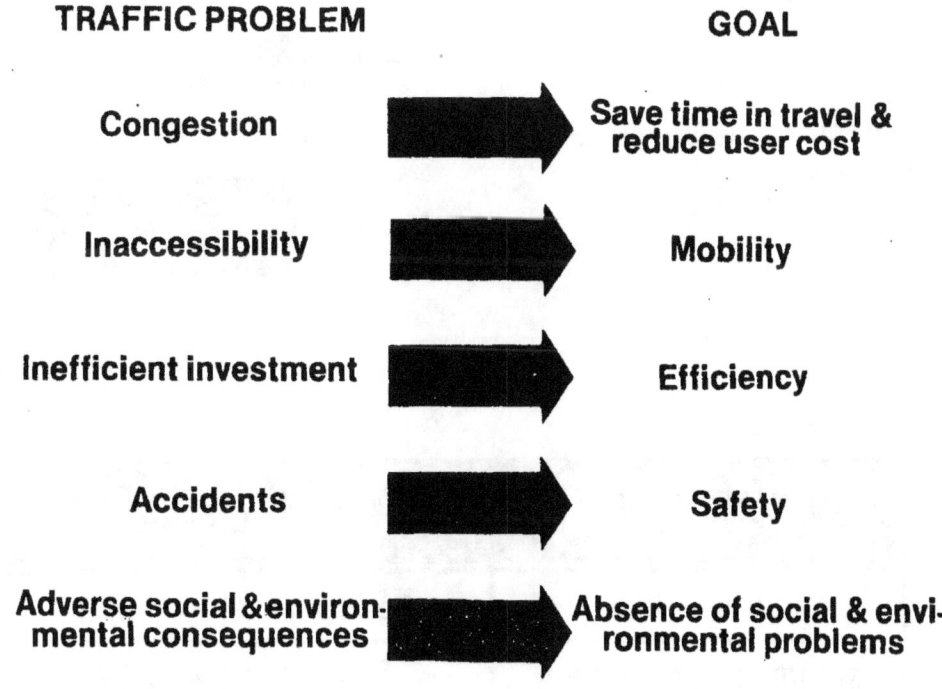

TRAFFIC PROBLEM	GOAL
Congestion	Save time in travel & reduce user cost
Inaccessibility	Mobility
Inefficient investment	Efficiency
Accidents	Safety
Adverse social & environmental consequences	Absence of social & environmental problems

PROBLEM:

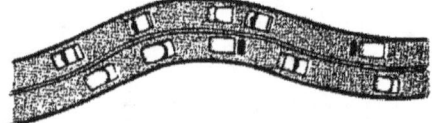

CONGESTION wastes time and increases operating costs.

CONGESTION — Motorists dislike traffic congestion primarily because of wasted time and the resulting increased operating costs. Excessive operating costs can be measured with a fair degree of precision. For example, on a I-mile free-flowing roadway of 30 miles-per-hour speed, three stops of 30-seconds duration each will result in an increase of approximately 90 percent in total running cost of the car. Measuring the value of a motorist's time is far more difficult. However, evidence shows that, given a choice, motorists will forfeit operating economy to save time.

GOAL: TO PROVIDE EFFICIENT TRAFFIC FLOW

ADEQUATE CAPACITY saves time and reduces operating cost.

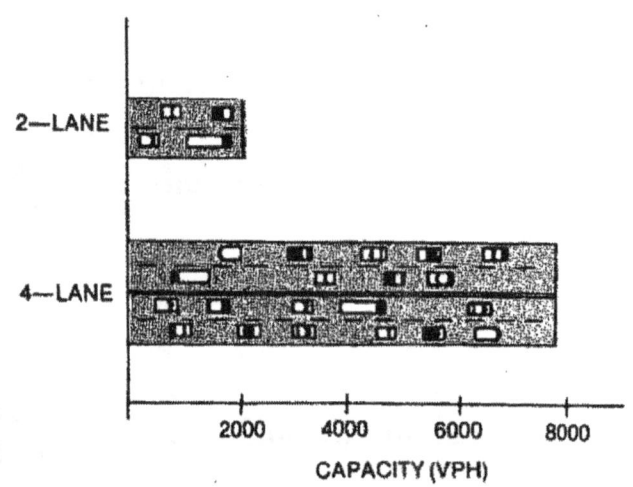

OBJECTIVE	INDICATOR
Cut travel time	Peak period travel time
Minimize congestion	Peak period volume
Reduce user cost	Vehicle user cost

PROBLEM:

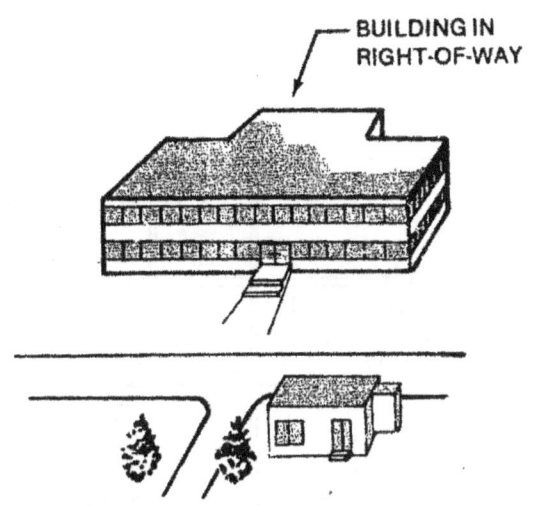

INACCESSIBILITY — Most people like to have the freedom to get where they want to go, when they want to go. High productivity is closely related to proximity in time. Without access, land cannot be developed and people cannot move to jobs, schools, hospitals, and so forth.

GOAL: TO IMPROVE MOBILITY OF POPULATION

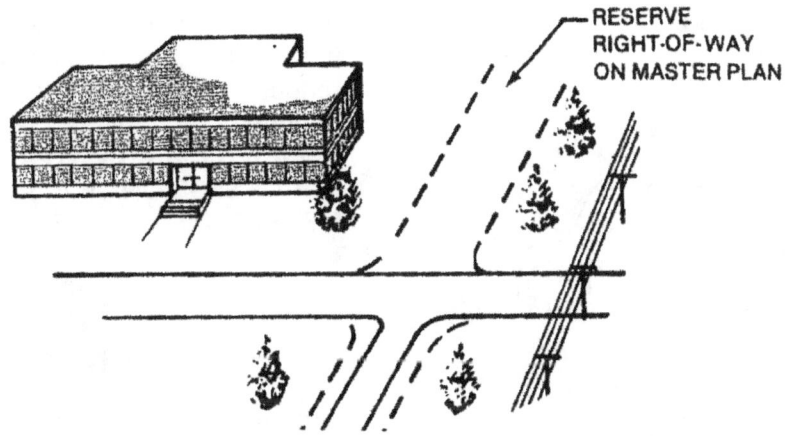

OBJECTIVE	INDICATOR
Reduce travel distance	Distance between point A and point B
Increase productivity of land and people	Changes in access caused by land development

PROBLEM:

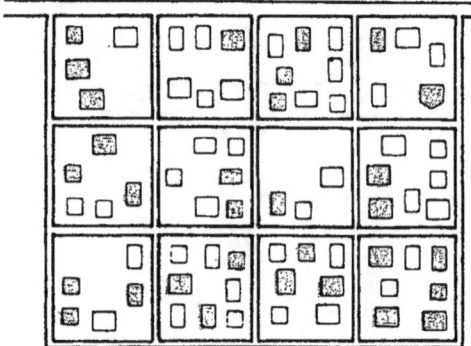

Where width of street, size of house, or size of lot is squeezed to a so-called "efficient minimum" — this is false economy.

INEFFICIENT INVESTMENT — Another universally condemned action is waste of public funds. The case of building unusable traffic facilities or misappropriating public funds is quite rare. However, the more frequent and important waste is that of false economy in traffic facilities. For example, decisions on expenditure are generally based on their budget appeal, not on their adequacy, such as patchwork improvements. The question of whether improvements may solve any particular problem is usually overlooked or avoided; example, a street-widening may prove inadequate the day it is completed and require immediate improvements. Another type of false economy results from so-called "efficient" planning, which creates waste. For example, in housing areas where the width of a street or the size of a house or the lot it occupies has been reduced to a so-called "efficient minimum" — this is false economy. EFFICIENT PLANNING IS MORE THAN AN OBSESSION TO SAVE; IT IS A METHOD TO IMPROVE.

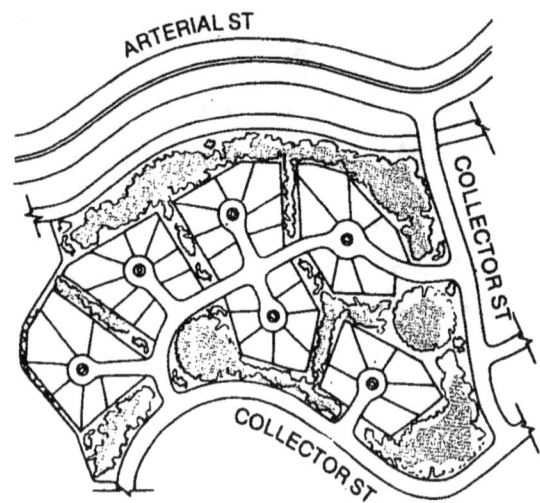

A modern residential street design preserves the neighborhood.

GOAL: TO ELIMINATE WASTE OF PUBLIC FUNDS AND PROTECT LIFE STYLE PATTERNS.

OBJECTIVE	INDICATOR
Decide expenditures based on adequacy, NOT budget appeal	Existing and desirable life-style patterns

PROBLEM:

ACCIDENTS — Accidents are the most significant of all traffic problems. In 1975 alone, approximately 58,800 motor vehicle accidents occurred on military installations, and resulted in an estimated cost of $70,000,000 to DOD and its personnel. Recent surveys of military installations revealed that the yearly accident rate ranged from 1 to over 40 per 1,000 people. This wide range indicates that the accident rate of an installation can be reduced through better traffic facilities.

ACCIDENT COST TO DOD
FATALITY — $287,175 per accident
PERSONAL INJURY — $8,085 per accident
PROPERTY DAMAGE — $520 per accident

GOAL: TO PROVIDE SAFE TRAVEL ROAD

The reduction of accidents on a four-lane divided highway is 29% over the undivided highway

FOUR-LANE UNDIVIDED — 4.09 accidents per million vehicle miles
VERSUS
FOUR-LANE DIVIDED — 2.91 accidents per million vehicle miles

OBJECTIVE	INDICATOR
Reduce accidents and fatalities	Number of accidents and fatalities

PROBLEM:

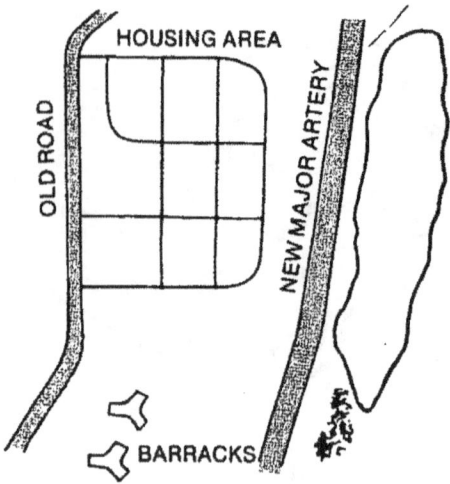

Noise Pollution.

SOCIAL AND ENVIRONMENTAL IMPACT — Ugliness, air pollution, strain, discomfort, noise, and nuisance are all components of the increasingly social nature of transportation problems. All of these problems are difficult to measure. Furthermore, problems such as ugliness are visual images that vary markedly among people, and hence it is difficult to obtain a consensus. The best way to consider these problems is in final plan selection.

GOAL: TO ENHANCE ENVIRONMENT

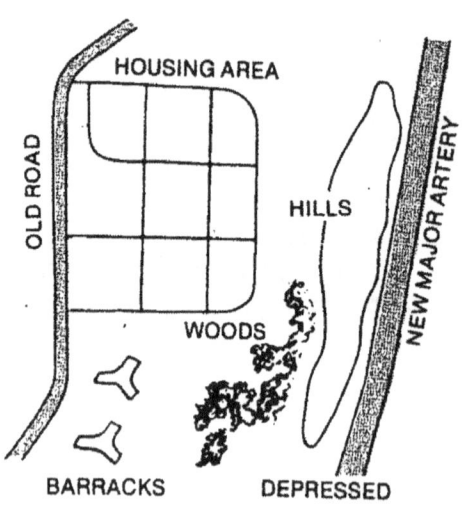

Built-In Noise Protection and Abatement

OBJECTIVE	INDICATOR
Minimize air/noise pollution	Exposure to pollution
Preserve open space	Recreational land available
Reduce travel on residential streets	Traffic volume on streets
Enhance views	Subjective judgment

BE AWARE OF CONFLICTS BETWEEN GOALS

Simply having an agreed set of goals and objectives is not enough because of the conflicts between goals. For example, the least expensive, initially, is to do nothing; whereas, the safest could very likely be the most expensive. Basically, goals should be listed and then screened to eliminate all but the most relevant. The goals selected should then be related to each other, so that losses toward one goal could be offset by gains toward another. Finally, these goals should be related to minimizing the total transportation costs.

III. PROCESS

SURVEYS

FORECAST

DEVELOPMENT

EVALUATION

IMPLEMENTATION

SURVEILLANCE AND REAPPRAISAL

THE ESTABLISHMENT OF A PLANNING PROCEDURE *is necessary in drafting a thoroughfare plan.* The process begins with a **review of existing facilities and travel characteristics. Data for present conditions** are then projected to the design year, and future deficiencies are noted. Based on these projections, **alternative improvements to present conditions** are evaluated, **a general thoroughfare plan** is selected, and **a priority schedule** is developed for implementation. The previous steps are continually reevaluated in view of the data developed at each succeeding step.

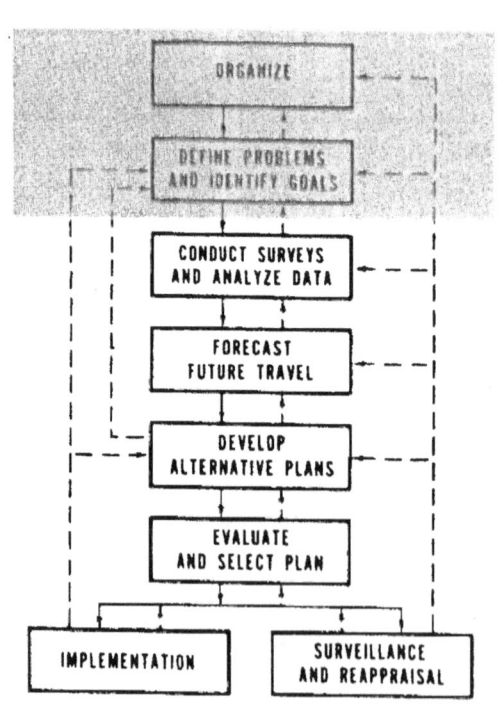

The cornerstone of the thoroughfare plan is the existing street system. Today's adequate street system, when projected to the design year, may become inadequate. The thoroughfare plan should lead to a design that will efficiently handle traffic volumes of the average weekday peak-traffic hours for the design year. These peak-hour flows usually are highly directional, with heavy inbound traffic in the morning and heavy outbound traffic in the evening. Occasionally, other time periods will determine a design for community service and retail-facility areas.

SURVEYS

SURVEYS are conducted to gather data on the present condition and traffic characteristics of an installation's roadways. These **data** are **analyzed** to estimate the traffic demands on the roadways and, as necessary, to redesign, evaluate, and program a road system to meet those demands.

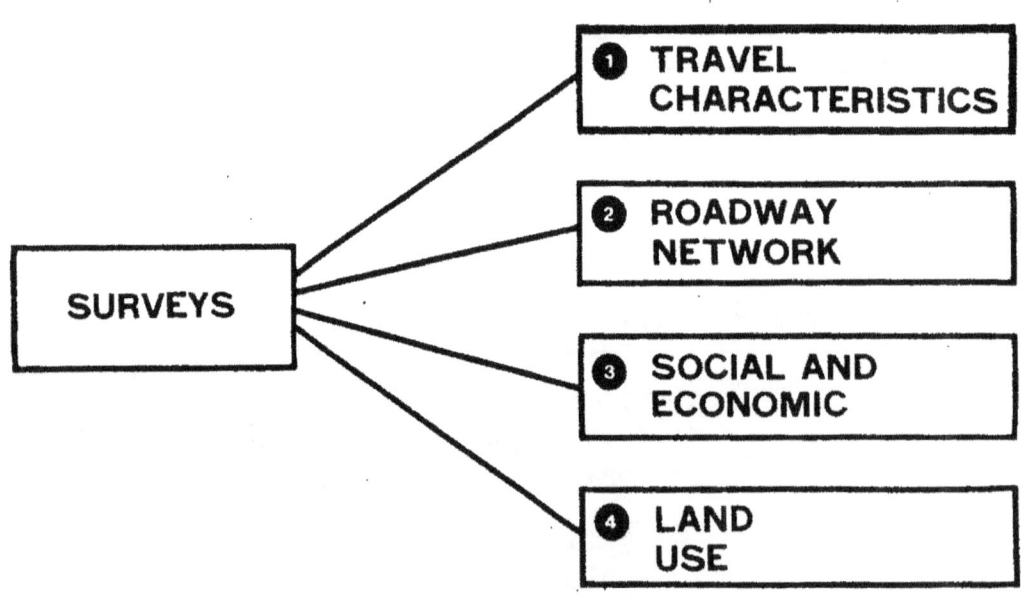

① TRAVEL CHARACTERISTICS

These surveys determine how many people use the road system, who they are, and their travel patterns. Data are gathered primarily from studies on traffic volume, vehicle occupancy, travel time and delay, and trip origin and destination. Of major interest to the installation thoroughfare planner is the employee home-to-work trip.

ESTABLISHES ROAD USAGE

② ROAD NETWORK

These surveys determine the condition and capacity of the roadway. Enough detail should be collected about the physical and operating characteristics of each segment of the route to calculate its capacity, as well as to determine its general level of service and accident history.

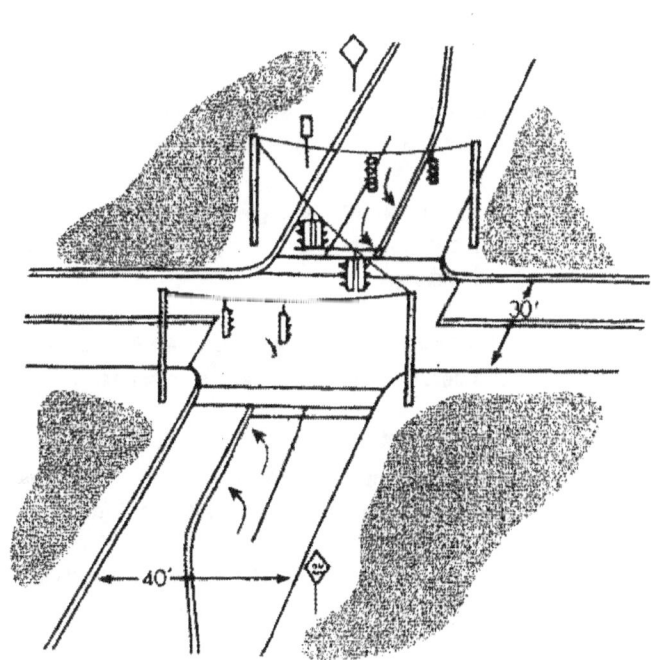

ESTABLISHES ROAD CONDITIONS

❸ SOCIAL AND ECONOMIC

These surveys establish past and present facts about the installation road user. Typical data collected include population, employment, duty hours, housing, social services, security measures, and carpool programs. These data are used primarily as a basis for forecasting growth potential. The data are used also for origin and destination surveys and as variables to determine trip generations.

ESTABLISHES ROAD USER CHARACTERISTICS

❹ LAND USE

Land patterns delineate the function of the land and are basic factors in determining traffic demands of an installation.

A simplified land-use classification system should include at least five categories:

RESIDENTIAL — single-family housing, apartment housing, bachelor officer and enlisted quarters.

ADMINISTRATIVE AND COMMERCIAL — offices, training centers, and exchanges.

INDUSTRIAL AND OPERATIONAL — maintenance and production facilities, ranges, motorpools, airports, and waterfront facilities.

COMMUNITY SERVICE — dependent schools, parks, churches, and recreational facilities.

OPEN SPACE — undeveloped acreage, forest, and streams.

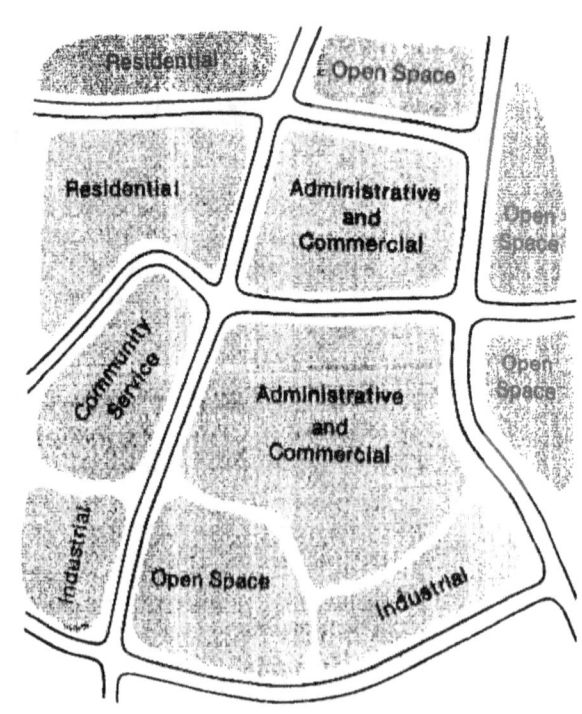

DELINEATES LAND FUNCTION

FORECAST

TRAVEL FORECASTS *are used to determine the transportation service NEED that will result from a change in land use.* For example, what roads will be needed to service a new housing area. Travel forecasts can include home-based, nonhome-based, work, nonwork, person, vehicle, and other type trips. Therefore, **the key to reducing the complexity of a travel forecast** *is to limit the forecast to only what is NEEDED to establish the maximum travel demand.* At a military installation, maximum travel demand is generally created by the highly directional employee home-to-work vehicle-trip that occurs during the morning or evening peak rush hour. Travel forecasts often need to establish only this type demand. A notable exception to this criterion is facilities that generate large traffic volumes not associated with the work trip, such as commercial and community facilities.

TRAVEL FORECASTS QUANTIFY FUTURE TRAFFIC DEMAND

THE FORECAST PROCESS starts with the **proposed road network and land use**, along with a **thorough understanding of existing traffic flow patterns.** Based on this information, **a prediction** is made of the number of future trips to and from an activity **(trip generation)**, where these trips begin and end **(trip distribution)**, and over which routes the trips are to be made **(trip assignment).** This process is then used to **evaluate** various alternative road systems. After each numerical evaluation, all forecasts are examined to determine if they are reasonable. If the forecast is unreasonable, the assumptions and procedures used to predict the trips should be reexamined and appropriate changes made.

SURVEYS
Existing Conditions

① LAND USE
Where will activities and roads be located?

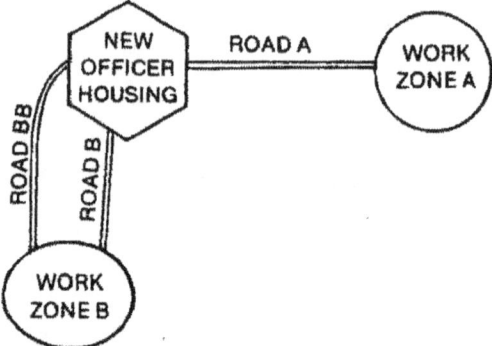

② TRIP GENERATION*
How many trips begin and end at the activity?

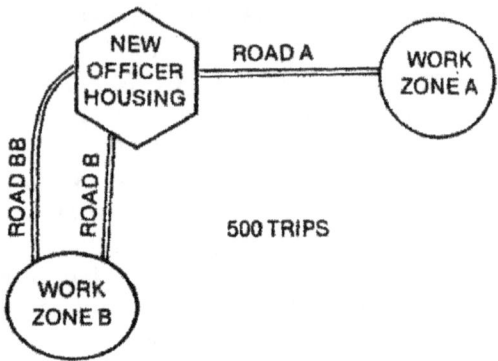

③ TRIP DISTRIBUTION*
How many trips will be made between activities?

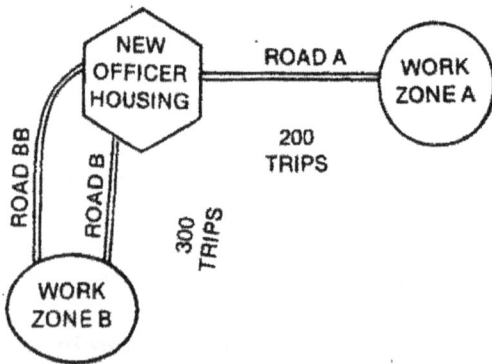

④ TRIP ASSIGNMENT*
Over which routes will trips between activities be made?

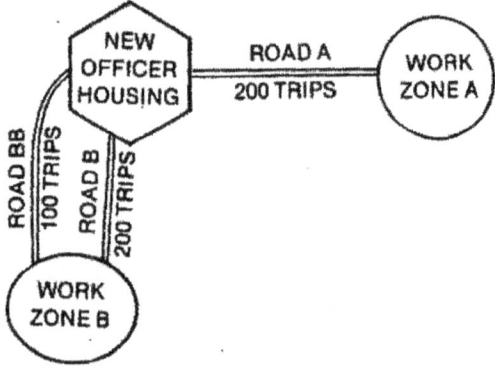

*Only peak-hour trips in direction of maximum flow are shown.

TRAVEL PROJECTIONS

1 LAND USE — Where will activities be located?

LAND-USE FORECASTS *provide estimates of future land development — location and type. These estimates* include not only *land usage,* but also *socio-economic variables, such as population, dwelling units, retail sales.* On military installations, this information is obtained from the installation master development plan. However, a major consideration in selecting locations shown on the development plan is the accessibility of that location. Therefore, as the road system is developed, proposed land uses shown on the development plan should be reexamined and changed, if necessary, to achieve a desirable future travel pattern. In every case, the road plan should provide a circulation system that maximizes access for movements between activities, giving due consideration to safety, comfort, and convenience, as well as cost.

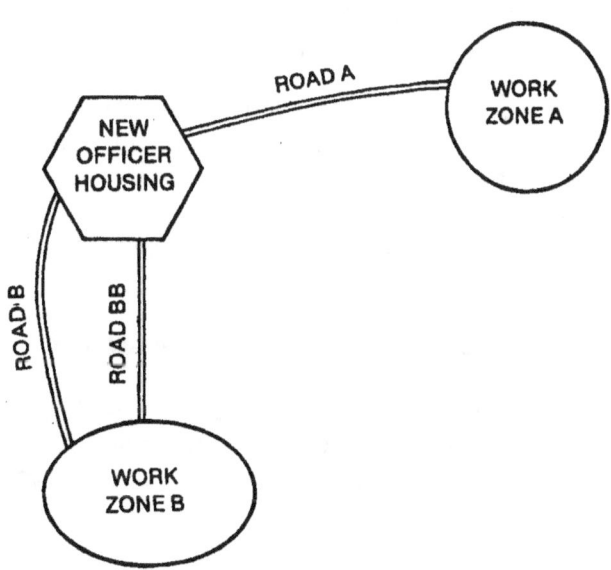

PREDICTIONS OF FUTURE TRAVEL ARE BASED ON FUTURE LAND USE

AND USE PLANNING OBJECTIVES

- Plan for people — not for automobiles and buildings.

- Arrange facilities to achieve the most attractive working and living environment.

- Improve internal traffic flow and external access.

- Consolidate various functional activities.

- Lay out commercial facilities in a way that will bring the patrons close to as many stores as possible once they have parked.

- Locate industrial sites adjacent to transportation facilities so that access is as convenient as possible.

- Provide space for future expansion of facilities and for offstreet parking.

- Locate pollution- and noise-emitting facilities away from residential and commercial areas.

- Route as much traffic as possible around dwelling areas.

- Separate pedestrian and vehicle flows.

- Provide locations that are convenient to residential areas for supplemental services — parks, schools, shops, and chapels.

② TRIP GENERATION — How many trips begin or end at an activity?

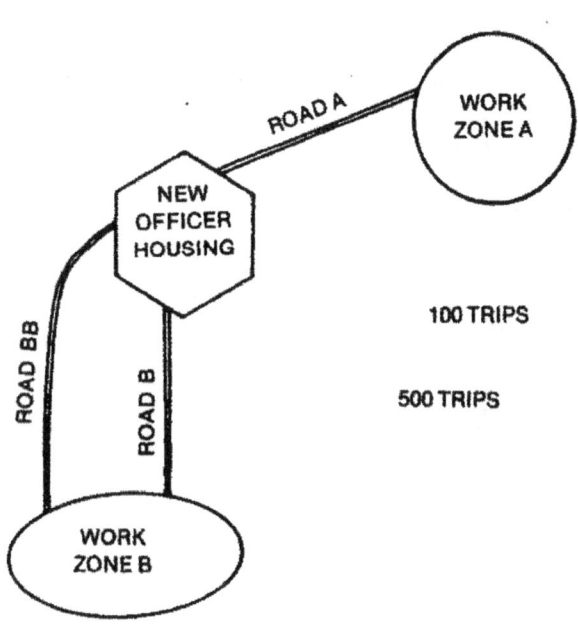

TRIP GENERATION DETERMINES PARKING AND ACCESS NEEDS

TRIP GENERATION ANALYSIS is a way to *estimate the number of future trips that will begin or end at an activity.* Trip generation analysis provides information on the peak volume of cars to be parked and the peak volume of traffic to be moved onto the road system at any one time.

Trip generation predictions are usually based on trip-making rates that are observed at existing facilities. Because of the many variables affecting traffic generation, specific generation rates have not been developed in this guide. However, for most military installations, trip-making rates can be determined from simple counts of vehicles entering and leaving driveways at existing similar facilities. When establishing generation rates, three characteristics of land use should be evaluated: intensity, character, and location of activity. "Intensity of land use" helps relate how many people will use the land and is expressed in such terms as "employees," "1,000 square feet of floor space," and "dwelling units." "Character of land use" refers to the type of land use, such as residential or industrial; whereas, "location of activity" generally refers to either a central built-up area or a remote area. When using existing facilities to estimate trip generation rates, both facilities should be similar in intensity, character, and location.

TYPICAL GENERATION UNITS

LAND USE	UNIT	LAND USE	UNIT
Bank	1,000 sq ft GFA*	Industrial	employee
Bank, drive-in	drive-in window	Institutional (schools)	student & employee
Barracks	person	Library	1,000 sq ft GFA*
Bowling alley	1,000 sq ft GFA*	Military installation	employee
Cafeteria	seat	Office building	employee
Chapel	seat	Recreation facilities	military strength
Clubs	member	Research facility	employee
Commercial	1,000 sq ft GFA*	Restaurant	seat
Dental clinic	dental chair	Service station	pump
Family housing	dwelling unit	Theater	seat
Golf club	member	Visitor center	employee
Guest house	bedroom	Warehouse	employee
Hospital	outpatient & employee	*Gross floor area	

EXAMPLE GENERATION*

A. **STATE PROBLEM AND NEED**

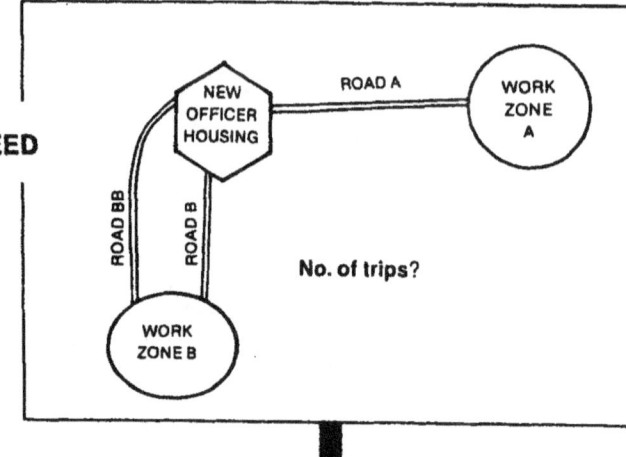

B. **IDENTIFY LAND-USE FACTORS**
- LOCATION
- CHARACTER
- INTENSITY

- BUILT-UP AREA
- RESIDENTIAL
- 500 HOUSES

C. **DEVELOP GENERATION RATE**
(Relation between trip making and land use at similar facility)

SURVEY AT SIMILAR FACILITY
- BUILT-UP AREA
- 400 HOUSES
- RESIDENTIAL
- 400 CARS EXITING IN PEAK HOUR
- TRIP RATE = 1.0 TRIPS/HOUSE

D. **APPLY RELATIONSHIP TO FORECAST**

- PEAK-HOUR ACCESS DEMAND = (500 HOUSES) (1.0 TRIPS/HOUSE)
  = 500 TRIPS

* Only peak-hour trips in direction of maximum flow are shown.

3 TRIP DISTRIBUTION — How many trips will be made between activities?

TRIP DISTRIBUTIONS *are analyzed to establish the number of trips that will be made between specific activity areas.* Two basic types of *mathematical models* are used to predict future trip distribution: *growth models and distribution models. Growth models* expand existing trips between zones based on an anticipated growth rate; whereas, *distribution models* estimate travel patterns based on the number of trips generated by the various zones, and then distribute these trips among the zones. The better known traffic models include the Fratar, Gravity, Intervening Opportunities, and Competing Opportunities. However, since these models require sophisticated data collection and analyses, they are not generally used at relatively small military installations.

TRIP DISTRIBUTION AT A MILITARY INSTALLATION generally can be *accomplished through* two methods. *An average-growth factor method* is used where significant changes in the zonal characteristics are not expected. When areas are almost completely undeveloped, a *proportional distribution method* is used. Both methods present reasonably accurate predictions of the future home-to-work trip. The average-growth method projects future trips between two zones by applying an average of the two zonal growth rates to the existing trips between the zones. On the other hand, the distribution method simply proportions the trips to be generated at a new facility in relation to existing concentrations at trip origins. Relationships for use in these models can be developed from origin and destination studies and/or peak-hour traffic counts.

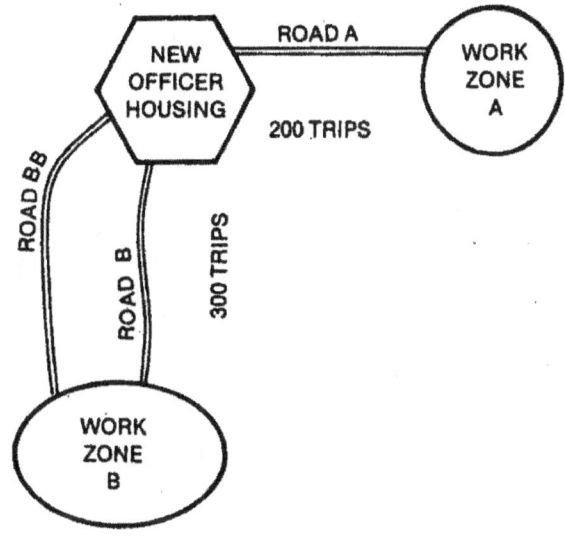

TRIP DISTRIBUTION DETERMINES TRAFFIC CORRIDOR

EXAMPLE DISTRIBUTION *

I. GROWTH MODEL

Where:

$$T_{ij} = t_{ij}\left(\frac{F_i+F_j}{2}\right)$$

T_{ij} = future trips between i & j
t_{ij} = existing trips between i & j
F_i = growth factor at i
F_j = growth factor at j

(A) DETERMINE NUMBER OF EXISTING TRIPS BETWEEN ZONES

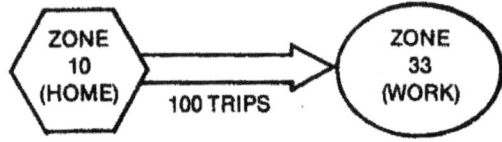

(FROM ORIGIN AND DESTINATION SURVEYS)

(B) ESTIMATE GROWTH RATES FOR BOTH ZONES

$$F_{10} = 1.6$$
$$F_{33} = 1.4$$

(INSTALLATION GROWTH ESTIMATES FROM MASTER DEVELOPMENT PLAN)

(C) COMPUTE FUTURE TRIPS

$$T_{10,33} = t_{10,33}\left(\frac{F_{10}+F_{33}}{2}\right)$$

$$= 100\left(\frac{1.6+1.4}{2}\right)$$

$$= 150 \text{ TRIPS}$$

II. DISTRIBUTION MODEL

Where:

$$T_{ij} = T_j\left(\frac{P_i}{\sum_{i=1}^{n} P_i}\right)$$

T_{ij} = future trips between i and j
T_j = future trips generated at j
P_i = existing trips produced at i
$\sum_{i=1}^{n} P_i$ = total trips produced

(A) DETERMINE TRIPS TO BE GENERATED AT NEW FACILITY

500 HOUSING UNITS WILL GENERATE 500 TRIPS

(B) FROM TRAVEL SURVEYS DETERMINE WHERE EXISTING TRIPS ARE DISTRIBUTED

(C) DISTRIBUTE FUTURE TRIPS PROPORTIONATELY

$$T_{4,2} = T_2\left(\frac{P_4}{P_4+P_{12}}\right)$$
$$= 500\left(\frac{400}{1000}\right)$$
$$= 200 \text{ TRIPS}$$

$$T_{12,2} = T_2\left(\frac{P_{12}}{P_4+P_{12}}\right)$$
$$= 500\left(\frac{600}{1000}\right)$$
$$= 300 \text{ TRIPS}$$

*Only peak-hour trips in direction of maximum flow are shown.

TRIP ASSIGNMENT — Over which routes will trips between activities be made?

The final phase of forecasting the travel demand is THE ASSIGNMENT OF VEHICLE TRIPS BETWEEN ZONES TO VARIOUS TRAFFIC ROUTES. One method of trip assignment is to simulate, from input on the travel pattern or desires of motorists, the extent to which a proposed system would be used. This technique is very complex; therefore, its use should be limited to those familiar with it.

On a military installation, the *primary technique for assigning traffic* is the *"all or nothing with capacity restraint."* In this technique, trips are allocated between zones to the one single path or route that represents the best path for a certain number of vehicles. Assignment thereafter is made to the second or next best alternate route. Frequently, the maximum traffic on a roadway is established as that capacity at which traffic can flow with only limited congestion, allowing the motorist to travel at his desired pace within legal limits. To achieve a balance in all zone-to-zone traffic, a trial-and-error assignment method generally is used; that is, minimum paths are calculated, assignments are made, roads are analyzed for travel comfort and convenience, then new assignments are made. This process continues until traffic is balanced on all routes between zones.

TRIP ASSIGNMENT DETERMINES ROAD WIDTH

FACTORS INFLUENCING ROUTE SELECTION

TANGIBLE	INTANGIBLE
Travel time	Human nature
Travel distance	Relative comfort and ease
Operating cost	
Frequency of stops	Esthetics
Safety	Geometrics

COMPONENTS OF ASSIGNED TRAFFIC

INDUCED TRAFFIC — new trips enticed

DIVERTED TRAFFIC — existing trips diverted from other paths

FACILITY-CREATED TRAFFIC — sightseers or traffic developed because of changes in land use

CONVERTED TRAFFIC — change in mode, such as bus to auto or auto-pool to driver

SHIFTED TRAFFIC — existing trips that show new origin and/or destination

NATURAL GROWTH TRAFFIC — result of natural growth rate

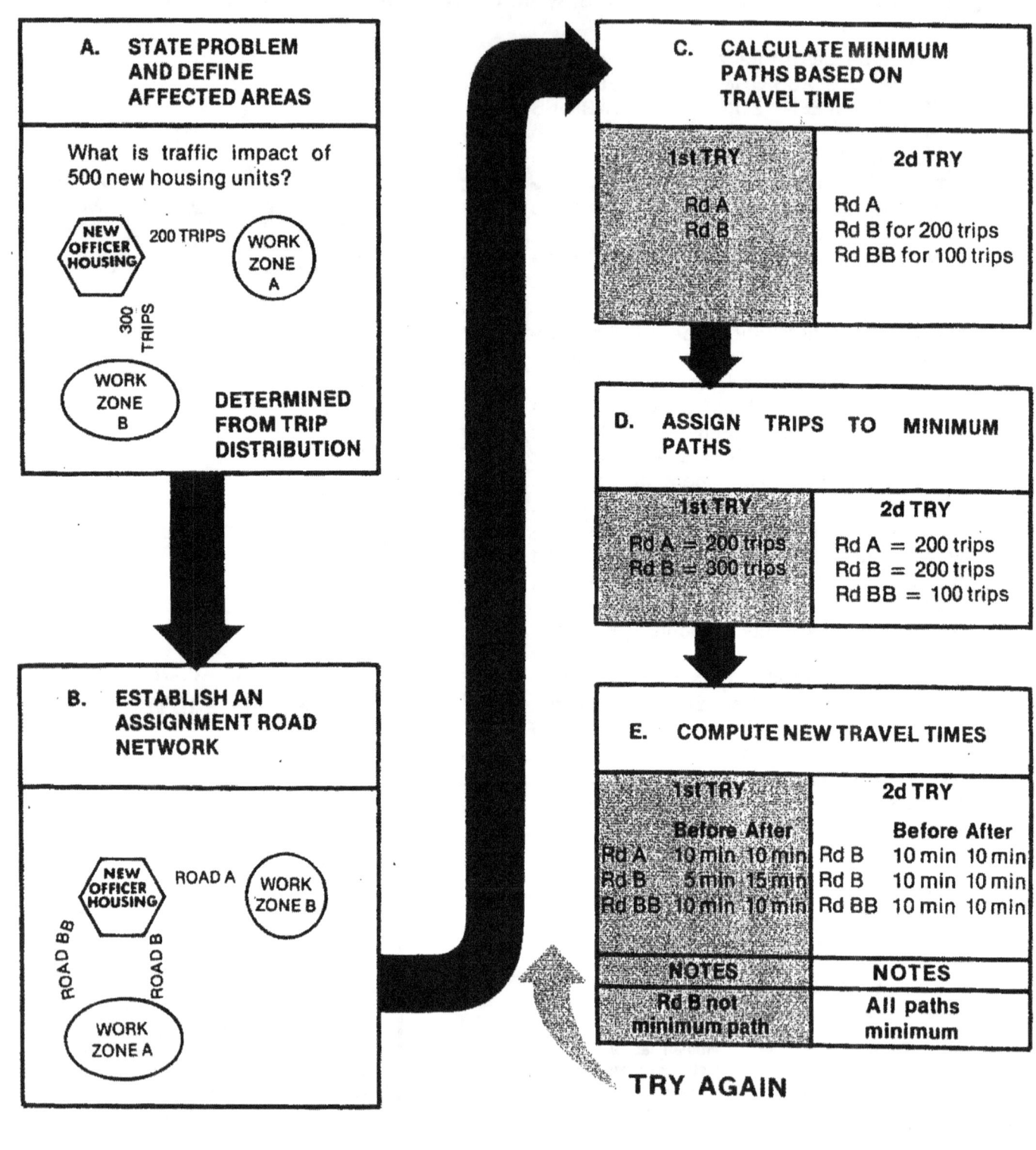

THIS PHASE OF ROAD DESIGN concerns **reducing traffic surveys and travel forecasts into various acceptable road systems.** The goal statements discussed in chapter 2 provide a basis for determining an acceptable system.

The development of alternatives, which by nature is a creative function, usually begins by estimating future travel on the existing road system. From these travel projections, problem areas and road needs can be identified. Assuming that this measure shows problems, a new trial road system is designed.

Once **one or more alternatives** are developed, the road plans are then tested to examine their performance. Congestion should be tested first. As alternatives pass the congestion test, they should be measured in more detail, such as travel time, travel distance, safety, parking, user costs, and environmental impact. The development and testing should end with a manageable number of alternatives that are acceptable in all phases of the roadway plan test. These alternatives then pass into the selection stage.

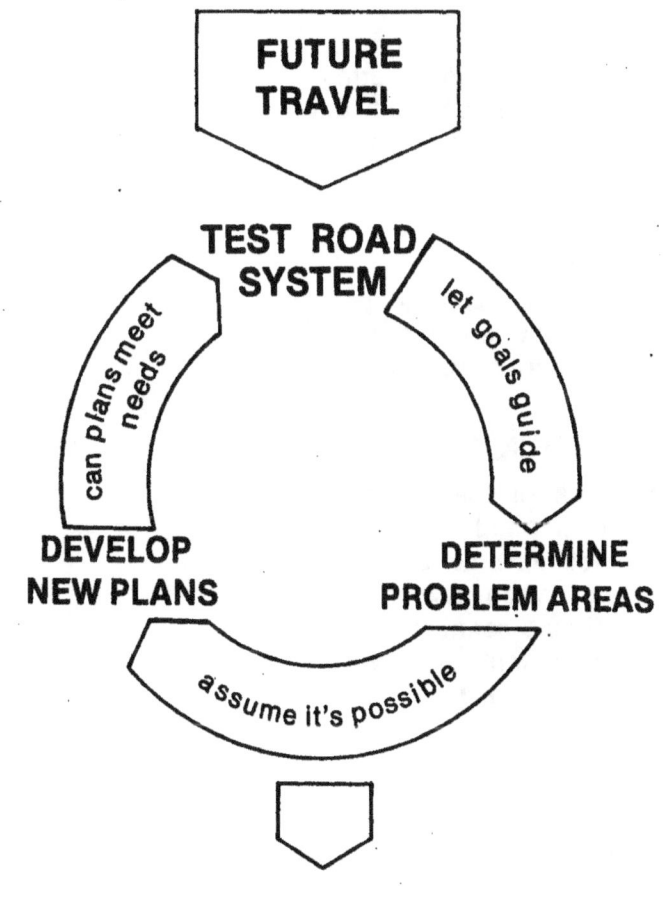

DEVELOPMENT OBJECTIVES

Although development is a creative function, the following objectives should be used to enhance the creative capacity of the road designer.

1 REDUCE CONGESTION

The test of any road system starts by measuring its capacity to handle projected traffic volumes. To eliminate capacity problems, the planner should not only insure that the congested roadways are improved, but should also consider improving remote routes in the vicinity, or even adding entire segments. For example, a bypass road can help relieve congestion on routes that are remote from it.

2 SERVE TRIP DESIRES

Analysis of vehicle trips — their origin, destination, length, and other characteristics — helps to determine installation roadway network, access-road needs, and entrance gate locations.

3 PROVIDE LAND-USE ACCESS

Alternate road systems should be developed to serve access needs identified by the installation master development plan.

4 PROVIDE SYSTEM CONTINUITY

Geometric configurations of the alternate road system should be limited to provide travel continuity, as well as practical construction and operation. When new routes are constructed, they should connect to the existing system where sufficient capacity exists to absorb the additional demand.

DEVELOPMENT OBJECTIVES

1. Reduce congestion
2. Serve trip desires
3. Provide land-use access
4. Provide system continuity

EVALUATION

IN THE EVALUATION, *all acceptable alternatives are considered and compared with one another to determine the best roadway plan.* The plan selected should provide the installation with a traffic corridor system that shows a road type or improvement for each traffic corridor. At this stage, the road plan does not show exact road location. However, each plan presented for evaluation has been found acceptable in the development phase, based on a preliminary look at the possibilities for location and design. In the evaluation phase, one plan is selected; then, in the implementation phase, the final plan is refined to show roadway location and design.

The most common method of evaluating a roadway is simply **to examine the measures of each alternative and make a judgment-based decision.** This decision usually requires trade-offs. For example, "X" minutes saved in travel are worth "Y" dwelling unit removals. As an aid in evaluating trade-offs, a weighting system applied to each evaluation criterion is suggested.

```
  ALTERNATIVE A                    ALTERNATIVE B

                    EVALUATION


                    BEST PLAN
                   ALTERNATIVE A
```

EVALUATION DETERMINES BEST PLAN

EVALUATION METHOD

① ESTABLISH CRITERIA

Accident rates
Travel time
Travel distance
Exposure to pollution

② DETERMINE WEIGHT OF EACH CRITERION

CRITERIA	WEIGHT
Accident rate	4
Travel time	3
Exposure to pollution	2
Travel distance	1

③ SPECIFY RELATIVE PERFORMANCE OF EACH ALTERNATIVE IN EACH CATEGORY

CRITERIA	PERFORMANCE RATING	
	ALT A	ALT B
Accident rate	2	1
Travel time	2	1
Exposure to pollution	1	2
Travel distance	1	2

④ MULTIPLY THE WEIGHT OF EACH CRITERION BY THE PERFORMANCE RATING, THEN SUM PRODUCTS

CRITERIA	ALT A WEIGHT × PERFORMANCE = PRODUCT RATING	ALT B WEIGHT × PERFORMANCE = PRODUCT RATING
Accident rate	4 × 2 = 8	4 × 1 = 4
Travel time	3 × 2 = 6	3 × 1 = 3
Exposure to pollution	2 × 1 = 2	2 × 2 = 4
Travel distance	1 × 1 = 1	1 × 2 = 2
Total	17	13

⑤ SELECT BEST PLAN

ALT A

IMPLEMENTATION

ROADWAY IMPLEMENTATION includes location, design, right-of-way acquisition, and construction. It is not a part of the roadway planning process. Planning is only a tool for making decisions today that will meet the roadway needs of tomorrow. However, continual planning provides data and assistance for the implementation. For example, a major service is the supply of base data for locating and designing the roadway within the traffic corridor.

SURVEILLANCE AND REAPPRAISAL

ONE CHARACTERISTIC OF TRANSPORTATION PLANS is that the analysis of a few years ago may be almost obsolete today. Obsolescence of the transportation plan may be caused by changes in goals, shifts of emphasis among goals, changes in funding, changes in administration, and improvements in transportation planning. Obsolescence of the plan is also frequently caused by radical departure from some part of the plan. Each installation should monitor changes that affect the transportation plan and should estimate their effect on the validity of the plan, changing the plan as necessary.

TRAFFIC ENGINEERING

TRAFFIC ROUTE LAYOUT

CONTENTS

	Page
I. SYSTEMS	1
GRIDIRON	2
RADIAL	3
II. CLASSIFICATION	1
ARTERIAL	2
COLLECTOR	2
LOCAL	3
III. LOCATION	1
DEVELOPING ALTERNATIVES-TRAFFIC SERVICE	2
DEVELOPING ALTERNATIVES-THE ENVIRONMENT	4
EVALUATION	5

TRAFFIC ROUTE LAYOUT

I. SYSTEMS

GRIDIRON

RADIAL

GOOD STREET SYSTEMS follow one of two basic patterns, or a combination of the two. One is the **GRIDIRON** pattern; the other, a **RADIAL-CIRCUMFERENTIAL** pattern.

Most military installations show a gridiron pattern, with traffic corridors extending outward from the central area. The headquarters and/or administrative units remain the major traffic generators. Any major shopping facilities are usually located adjacent to an arterial and, compared with administrative units, generate an insignificant amount of peak-hour traffic.

GRIDIRON PATTERNS COMMONLY FORM STREET SYSTEMS

GRIDIRON

The gridiron system, resembling a checkerboard, *is a series of streets located at approximate right angles to each other.* These streets produce blocks that are either *square or rectangular.*

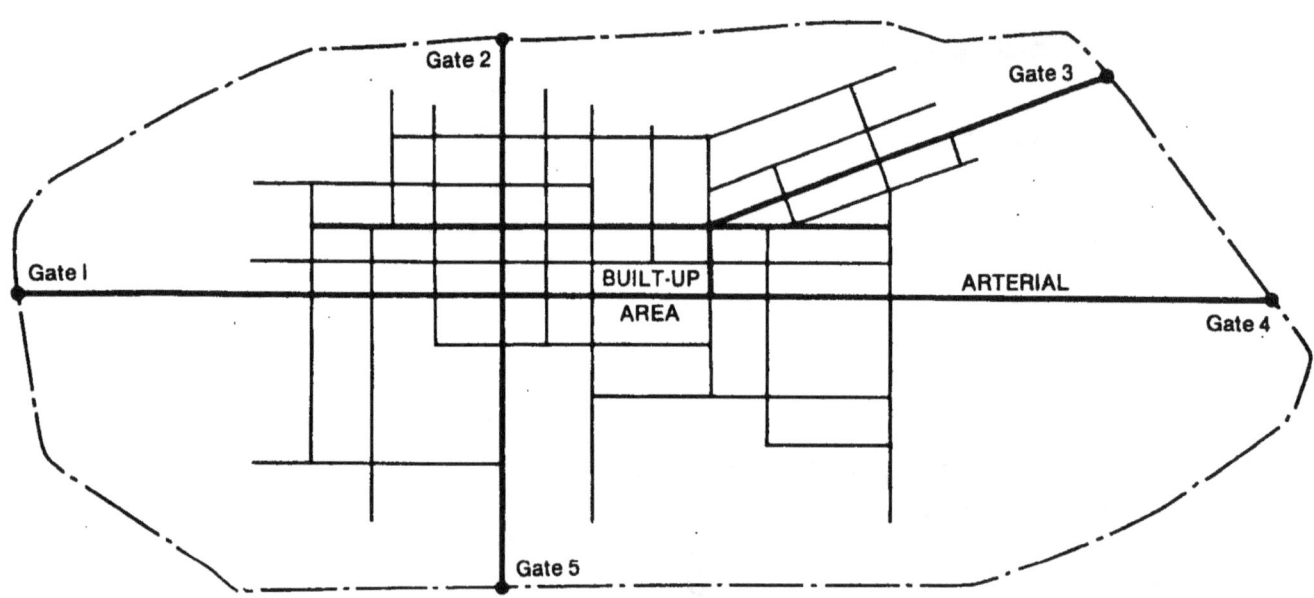

ADVANTAGES	DISADVANTAGES
Roads are easy to design and lay out. Roads can be extended indefinitely. Straight roads generally simplify the design of utilities. Rectangular blocks created by the street system are easy to subdivide. The street system is easily understood, named, and numbered.	The system does not adapt well to irregular topography. Travel between destinations located diagonally opposite each other is inconvenient and indirect. Most of the streets must be designed for high-volume traffic and have heavy-duty pavement, because every street is a through street and therefore capable of developing into a major thoroughfare. Shifting traffic and general dispersion of through traffic can spoil the entire area for best residential use, with little compensation in convenience or directness.

LOCAL

ALL ROADWAYS that are not classified as either arterial or collector are classified as LOCAL STREETS — that is, RESIDENTIAL and BUSINESS/INDUSTRIAL. *The chief function* of these streets is *to provide direct access to abutting land and to the higher road systems.* Local streets should not be developed as major traffic streets.

RESIDENTIAL STREETS

THE CHIEF PURPOSE OF RESIDENTIAL STREETS *is to provide access to housing units, as well as to serve as a channel for local utilities.* Therefore, they should be designed so that they will not become thoroughfares or major streets. They should be short and should follow the topography. Many are cul-de-sac, dead-end, or loop streets.

As its function is to serve abutting property, the residential street should be designed not to carry high-volume traffic, but to adequately meet the needs of the abutting property. The average traffic volume for a residential street varies from 250 to 500 vehicles per day, with a maximum volume of approximately 2,000 vehicles per day.

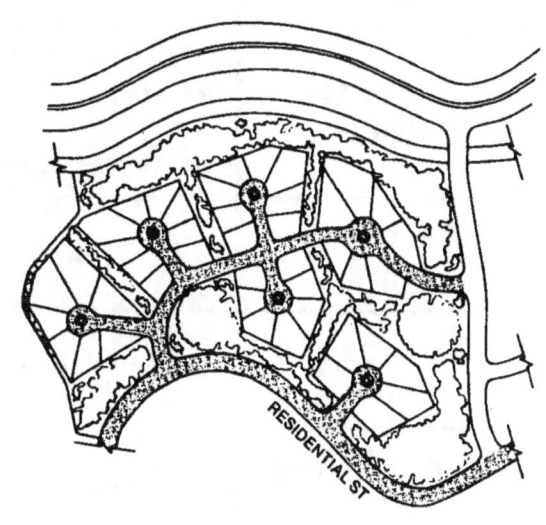

BUSINESS AND INDUSTRIAL STREETS

BUSINESS-AREA STREETS *serve business-area traffic.* These streets should be designed to permit easy movement from one location of the business area to another and to and from entrance gates.

INDUSTRIAL STREETS *serve abutting property as well as vehicular traffic.* These streets are used frequently by large commercial vehicles; therefore, the accumulation of trucks and peak-hour employee movements should be given particular consideration.

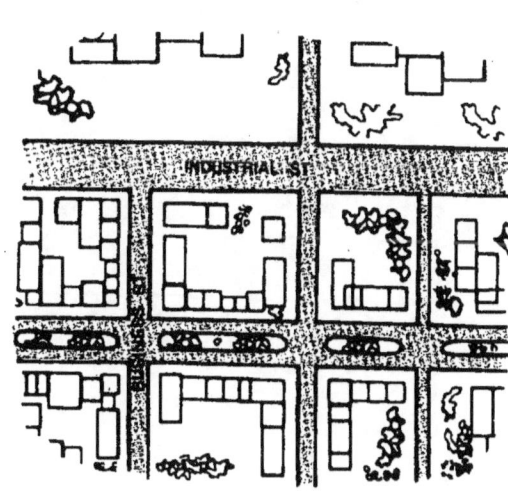

GUIDELINES FOR CLASSIFICATION

CRITERIA	ARTERIAL	COLLECTOR	LOCAL
Trip Length (mi)	1–3	1	1/2
Traffic Volume (vpd)	8,000–25,000	2,000–8,000	Less than 2,000
Service to Activities	High Volume Generators (Should not penetrate neighborhoods)	Local Areas Neighborhoods	Individual Sites
Spacing (mi)	1/4–2	1/8–1/2	NA
Access Control	Limited - Extensive	None	None
Service to Through Traffic	Moderate - High	Low	Low

II. CLASSIFICATION

ARTERIAL

COLLECTOR

LOCAL

THE CLASSIFICATION OF ROADS BY TYPE *is necessary for communication among engineers, administrators, and the general public.* Different classification methods are used for different purposes. One method commonly used for military installations divides the road system into four general categories based on their relative importance: primary, secondary, tertiary, and patrol roads. For planning, the main considerations for classifying roads are travel desires of the road user, land service needs based on existing and expected future land use, and the overall road-system continuity. Therefore, the functional classification used in this guide divides roadways into three groups by function: arterial, collector, and local. Each group carries a set of suggested minimum design standards. These standards are in keeping with the importance of the roadway system and are governed by the specific service the system is expected to provide.

DISTRIBUTION OF STREET MILEAGE

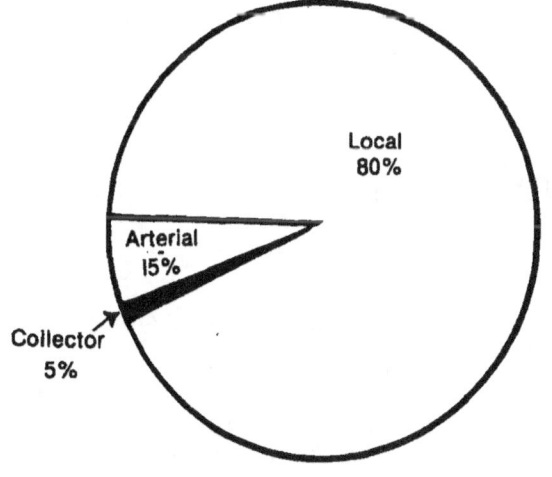

ARTERIAL

THE ARTERIAL SYSTEM may be of several types, depending on the size of the installation, but *the fundamental objective is the same for all: to move large volumes of traffic as safely and quickly as possible*. By design, the arterial system should carry a high volume of the total area traffic over a minimum mileage, without serving abutting property.

In their ultimate development, *arterials* may be either *freeways or expressways*. Freeways have only grade-separated intersections and prohibit access to abutting property. Expressways may have at-grade intersections, but they, too, usually prohibit land access.

At most military installations, *arterials are simply existing streets that place more emphasis on high-level traffic service than on land access.*

Arterial traffic volumes generally range from 8,000 to more than 20,000 vehicles per day. These roadways should be designed for a minimum of four and a maximum of six traffic lanes. When the traffic volume substantially exceeds 20,000 vehicles per day, some of the traffic should be diverted to another roadway. If diversion is impracticable, grade separations will be required at major intersections. Furthermore, roadways with traffic volumes approaching 25,000 vehicles per day will normally warrant a design for six traffic lanes and a median.

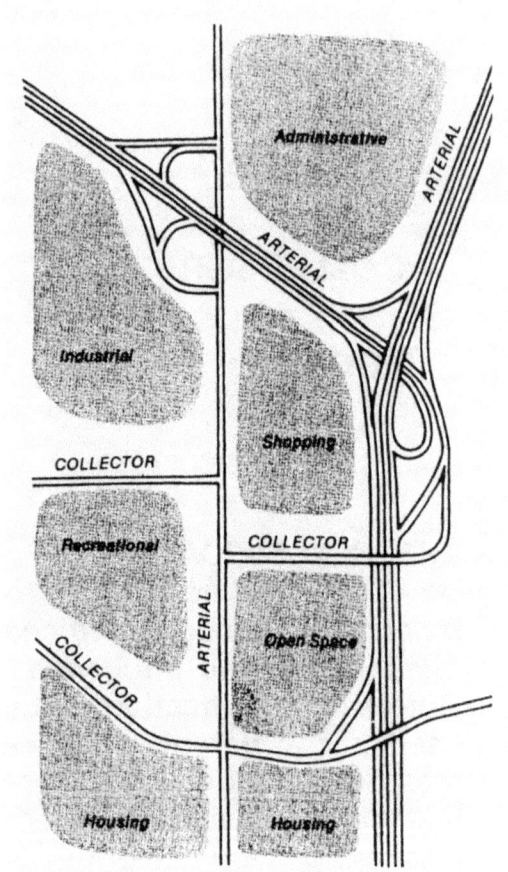

COLLECTOR

THE PRIMARY PURPOSE OF COLLECTOR STREETS *is*, as the term implies, *to collect traffic from the residential or commercial areas and move it to or from the arterial streets. These streets are of several types, but generally are of the same classification* since they all serve abutting property and carry traffic of a type different from that of local streets. Collector streets carry traffic volumes ranging from 2,000 to 8,000 vehicles a day and should have from two to four traffic lanes.

RADIAL

THE RADIAL-CIRCUMFERENTIAL SYSTEM consists of *a series of major streets radiating from the central, or built-up, area of an installation.* These radials are supplemented *by a series of circumferential streets that encircle the built-up area.* With such a street system, it is very important to have an inner loop around the built-up area — because, if all radial streets were to cross at one point in the built-up area, intolerable congestion would result. With an inner loop, traffic can flow on the radials toward the built-up area, then follow the loop around the built-up area to a point opposite its destination; it can then turn into or toward its built-up area destination. Usually, the radials terminate at the inner loop, except one or two in each major direction cross the built-up area. The built-up area usually is a gridiron pattern, which best serves built-up area traffic.

RADIAL STREETS provide direct travel between the outskirts and the built-up area of an installation. These routes adapt easily to topography and, therefore, usually are established quite naturally except where prevented by deliberate planning.

CIRCUMFERENTIAL STREETS, on the other hand, permit travel from one point to another in the outskirts of the installation without going through the built-up area. The alignment of circumferential streets, like radial streets, usually is either irregular or straight, not circular as the term implies.

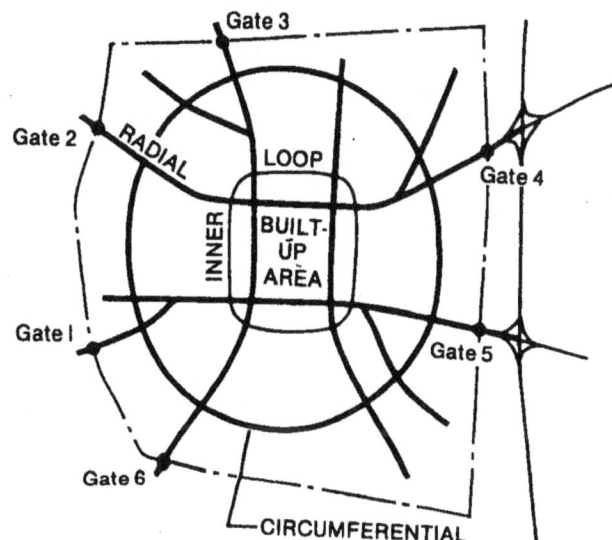

ADVANTAGES	DISADVANTAGES
Travel between any two points on an installation usually can be more direct. The system design permits good adaptation of the streets to the topography. A major street can be easily distinguished from a minor street. Each street is designed for one particular purpose, which leads to traffic stability. Cost savings in street construction and maintenance programs can result, because this system requires less actual street mileage than the gridiron requires.	Streets are more difficult to layout than in the gridiron system. Street layout leaves irregularly shaped parcels of land that may be hard to subdivide. Road layout complicates utility installations. Development of circumferential streets, which relieve congestion in the built-up area, is often neglected.

ROAD SYSTEM OBJECTIVES
Concentrate most of the traffic on a few well-designed arterial roads.
Locate arterial roads to serve the built-up area.
Supply an adequate number of nonarterial streets.
Provide direct travel from entrance gates to work areas.
Insure compatible related land use.

III. LOCATION

DEVELOPING ALTERNATIVES

TRAFFIC SERVICE

THE ENVIRONMENT

EVALUATION

THE PURPOSE OF THE ROAD LOCATION PROCESS *is to position a road within a strip of land in such a way that it will satisfy traffic demands and environmental considerations.* This process starts with *route requirements* and *selected traffic corridors identified in the planning process.* From this information, alternative road locations are prepared and evaluated. The best alternative is then selected. The process takes place after the planning phase and prior to the design phase, but blends into both.

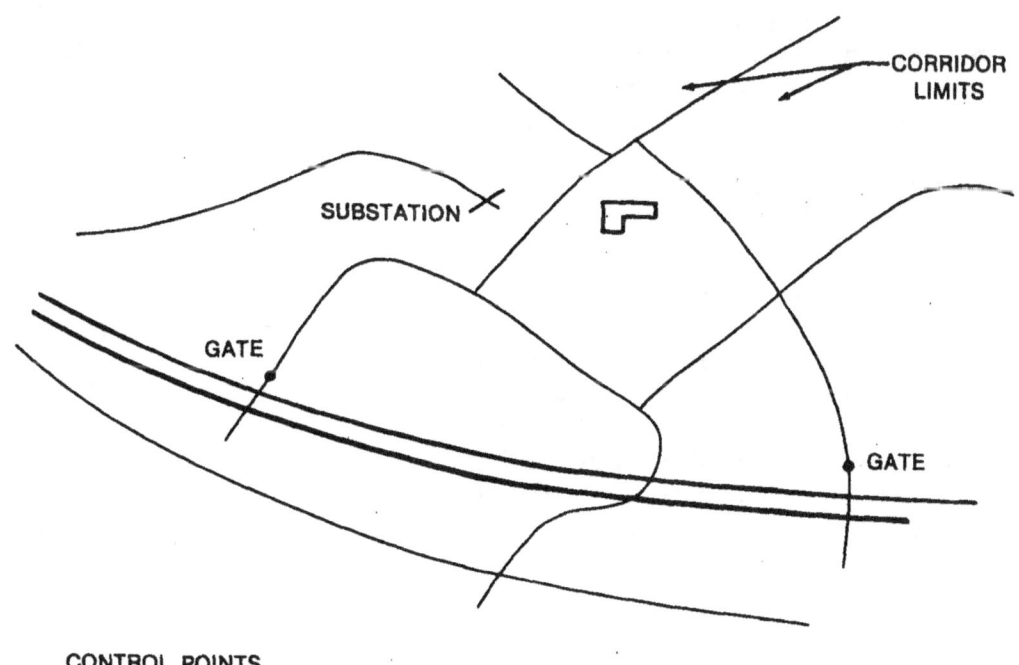

CONTROL POINTS

DEVELOPING ALTERNATIVES

THE TRAFFIC SERVICE

- IDENTIFY CONTROL POINTS AND CORRIDOR LIMITS.
- IDENTIFY TRAFFIC DESIRES.
- PLACE TRIAL LINES ON MAP.
- LAY OUT TURNING MOVEMENTS AT CROSSROADS.
- ESTIMATE NUMBER OF TRAVEL LANES.
- REVISE ALIGNMENT FOR OPERATIONAL IMPROVEMENTS.

IDENTIFY CONTROL POINTS AND TRAFFIC CORRIDOR LIMITS

The first step in the location process is to identify as many control points as possible within a traffic corridor. **A traffic corridor** *is a strip of land through which a road can be developed to satisfy traffic demands and environmental considerations.* Control points include such features as streets to be intersected, buildings to be retained, environment to be protected, parks and recreational areas to be maintained, and residential and industrial areas to be developed. Information for this step is generally developed in the planning process.

IDENTIFY TRAFFIC DESIRES

Provision of service for the estimated and assigned volumes is a **major control of location design.** Forecasted traffic largely determines the type of roadway required; whereas, the general desire lines of traffic indicate the preferred location.

DEVELOPING ALTERNATIVES IS LARGELY TRIAL AND ERROR

PLACE TRIAL LINES ON MAP

Once traffic assignments and the location of major traffic generators are known, a trial line for through movements should be superimposed over a map of the corridor. The initial trial line should connect the topographic and development control points, as well as conform to the general direction of the true traffic desires.

LAY OUT TURNING MOVEMENTS AT CROSSROADS

The selection of crossroads to be intersected or interchanged is usually done *concurrently with or following the initial layout.* Good main line operating characteristics favor widely spaced connections, uniform intersection design, and continuity of the through traffic. Spacing between connecting roads should safely accommodate weaving, turning movements, and signal progression. As a "rule of thumb," **minimum spacing of intersections on arterials should be 400 to 500 feet, and on collector streets, 300 feet.**

With general alignment and connecting crossroads chosen, the next step is to design turning movements. The design should provide a high level of service and safety not only to turning traffic, but also to through traffic. This can be done by designing for uniformity of turning movements and for continuity. **A standard intersection design should be developed and consistently applied except for the extreme cases.** Furthermore, for continuity, every attempt should be made to allow through traffic to flow naturally without being confronted with decision points.

ESTIMATE NUMBER OF TRAVEL LANES

After a trial line and turning movements have been drawn out, **the number of lanes should be estimated.** This estimation is based on design traffic volumes that will allow the driver to operate his vehicle on the road with certain minimum speeds, maximum traffic densities, and vehicle delay. For initial location, the roadway should be divided into segments of relatively uniform conditions. Two-directional traffic forecast for each segment can then be divided by the design traffic volume for that type of highway and rounded to the next higher even number of lanes. Given this estimated number of lanes and the type of roadway, the width of right-of-way necessary to construct the roadway cross section can be estimated. This width of land needed should be estimated for each alternative so that the land, improvements taken, and cost involved can be identified.

REVISE ALIGNMENT FOR OPERATIONAL IMPROVEMENTS

After completion of the location layout, **the proposed roadway should be reviewed for possible operational improvements.** The adequacy of turning, merging, weaving, capacity, and spacing should be reevaluated. Frequently, the layout of the number of lanes and turning movements may show a need to change the intersection location in order to eliminate or add an intersection to satisfy user service.

4

DEVELOPING ALTERNATIVES-THE ENVIRONMENT

The previous discussion concerned locating a roadway where it would provide safe, efficient, and economical transportation. However, it is also necessary to consider *the roadway as an element of the total environment. Roadways can and should be located and designed in a way that will complement their environment.*

TYPICAL ENVIRONMENTAL CONSIDERATIONS

Hold heavy cut and fill to a minimum. The roadway that flows with the topography will minimize erosion and sedimentation problems.

Evaluate soil strength and settlement information to identify potential problem areas.

Locate roadways to enhance accessibility of natural areas.

Locate roadways to minimize stream crossings and channel changes.

Mark corridor maps to portray such factors as land use, soil drainage, vegetation, wildlife preservation, surface and ground water, and potential recreation areas.

Avoid noise-sensitive areas altogether, or reduce noise effects through buffer zones, restrictions on truck traffic, avoidance of long and steep grades, or other special construction measures.

Make location decisions that will aid in the control and reduction of traffic-generated air pollution and energy consumption.

Locate new roadways, where feasible, in alignment with established geometric patterns.

Minimize disruptions of residential neighborhoods, schools, parks, shopping areas, industrial complexes, and medical centers.

Preserve areas of historical or architectural value.

Consider retaining unique areas or those that should remain the focal point.

Include a citizen participation program as part of the planning and location process.

Consider the need for vehicle access, including emergency vehicles, to health services, residential areas, industrial areas, parks, commercial areas, and employment centers.

5

EVALUATION

THE BASIS FOR SELECTING ONE ROADWAY LOCATION OVER ANOTHER WITHIN THE SAME CORRIDOR *is a judgment as to the location that will best achieve the traffic goals of the installation.* **These goals include: reduced travel time and cost, increased safety, improved travel comfort and convenience, and desirable social and environmental development.** At small installations, many times an intuitive judgment is a sufficient basis for decisions. However, at large installations, this intuitive approach or the "try and see" approach is generally not practical because of the enormity and permanence of road works. A comprehensive evaluation is essential in these instances.

In the location evaluation process, it is necessary *to place values on the benefits, costs, and consequences associated with the alternatives considered.* Placing these values is obviously a difficult task. However, identifying and ranking the relevant evaluation criteria *help to increase the probability of achieving the optimal choice.*

A first step in ranking the various alternates *is through an economic evaluation.* Of course, the most economical route may not necessarily be selected as the "best" because of adverse social and environmental consequences. However, this evaluation will permit the decisionmaker to narrow the alternatives to the one that is "best" in monetary terms. Furthermore, *the economic evaluation can often be used to decide whether or not to proceed, defer, or terminate a project.* For example, if the economic evaluation indicates a high prospective rate of return or benefit to cost and if the social and environmental consequences are of minor importance, a decision can easily be made to authorize construction. For marginal projects, the decision to authorize construction will require that an environmental evaluation be made. This evaluation considers those factors that cannot be given a monetary value. Although this evaluation is usually quite arbitrary, the decisionmakers can rank all the elements involved, and thus, review and evaluate the factors in a systematic and equitable manner. *The guiding consideration* throughout the process *should be that the decisionmaker is making a decision on behalf of the public.* Therefore, **the best solution must consider what is right to the expert, then the consequences of implementation should be best for the average installation citizen.**

www.ingramcontent.com/pod-product-compliance
Lightning Source LLC
Chambersburg PA
CBHW082207300426
44117CB00016B/2698